Get Set for Media and Cultural Studies

Get Set for Media and Cultural Studies

Tony Purvis

Edinburgh University Press

UNIVERSITY OF CHICHESTER

Edinburgh University Press Ltd
22 George Square, Edinburgh

Typeset in Sabon
by Servis Filmsetting Ltd, Manchester, and
printed and bound in Great Britain by
William Clowes Ltd, Beccles, Suffolk

A CIP record for this book is available from the British Library

ISBN 0 7486 1695 0 (paperback)

CONTENTS

INTRODUCTION

ABOUT THIS BOOK

Before I started writing this book, I held a number of workshops and seminars with first- and second-year undergraduates studying for degrees in media and cultural studies at UK universities. The students, from a range of social, cultural and international backgrounds, were asked to discuss the kind of advice they would pass on to first-year students just starting a degree in media and/or cultural studies. During the writing of the book, I tested sections and chapters when students said they were finding parts of the degree challenging. However, from the workshops, two key points emerged. The first one was 'provide a sense of the span of media and cultural studies'. Students new to the field of media and cultural studies are amazed at the breadth and depth of material covered on degree programmes in these areas. The second point was 'make links between what we learn in modules and the study skills required in media and cultural studies degrees'. The students I spoke to said they really benefited from having a clear and detailed idea about such things as essay writing, seminar presentations, doing media production projects and the recent debates about employability and progress files. It is undergraduates' responses such as these which helps shape the current volume in the Get Set series.

This book will be of interest to:

- readers who are about to embark on or have already started a degree course in media and cultural studies;
- those who are interested in media studies and cultural studies and want to know more about the subjects;
- students who are interested in study and research skills.

The book encourages you to understand how to approach critically and enthusiastically media and cultural studies. In addition, the book will help you in the development of important critical and research skills in media and cultural studies, inviting you to ask questions, and think analytically about the media and cultural industries.

RESISTING EASY ANSWERS

Two of the most pressing questions for all new students concern the programme of study and what it will entail. The book attends to these questions in a number of ways, but it answers the questions specifically in relation to media and cultural studies. Another important question – one which is often asked in essays and examinations, and which preoccupies students at the start of the course – is concerned with the terms 'media' and 'culture'. What is meant by 'the media' and media studies; and what is meant by 'culture' and cultural studies? Do the definitions matter? Read on – carefully! In the study of media and culture, perhaps hard-and-fast definitions of the terms are to be avoided and resisted. This book will not provide them, at least not in order to stifle or conclude ongoing debates. Many degree programmes will also resist these definitions and deliberately encourage some complexity across the first year of study. Such complexity is to be welcomed rather than rejected!

APPROACHES

Questions and confusions about degree programmes have in part resulted in this series of books. The Get Set series aims to encourage and invite students to explore the study skills, the learning strategies and the topics and themes involved in studying for a degree programme. *Get Set for Media and Cultural Studies* also aims to encourage its readers to ask questions about how to approach study skills and degree topics *critically* rather than provide definitions which ultimately prove of limited use. Many introductory textbooks concerned with summarising and outlining others' work will supply students with a range of responses, definitions and answers. It is true – at least to some extent – that several of the principal definitions of media and culture are considered in this book, and later sections provide a general discussion and an outline of methods of analysis in the study of media and culture. However, this is not a textbook in the sense in which the term is generally understood, and it does not offer neat summaries. But it does prompt you to ask questions, to think critically, to question the media and culture, and to adopt a positive and wholehearted approach to study and learning.

The book encourages you to consider how media and culture can be approached as fields of study at university. In pursuing this aim, *Get Set for Media and Cultural Studies* invites and expects readers to ask more questions, to consider key approaches to study, and to gain a confident sense of what it means to engage critically with media and cultural studies. Many textbooks provide guidelines on methods of analysis, on theories and on the application of theory, and they can be essential in the first year of study. Second- and third-year students then go on to read sources which deal with discussion and examination of the media and culture industries in more detailed, more specific and more focused ways. These 'advanced' texts are the kinds of sources which the majority of textbooks cite and encourage students to read. Often, however, textbooks do not have the space or remit to consider critical approaches to study and learning. More specifically, there are few books which deal with approaches to study and research in media and cultural studies at university. This current book addresses the questions students ask concerning successful, critical and reflexive study at university, specifically in relation to media and cultural studies.

DOING MEDIA AND CULTURAL STUDIES

One of the most frequently asked questions in the first year of study at university concerns introductory textbooks. It is often imagined that there will be one key text which will provide students with a complete knowledge base for the degree programme. However, a number of discoveries are made by undergraduates in the early months of study at university. Among these discoveries, which are made by media production students as much as media and cultural studies students, the following are the most frequently listed:

- There is no one book which covers the programme in its entirety.

- There is no 'right' answer to the essay question.

- I was told not to use 'I'.

- 'How' something happens is as important as 'why'.

- The question can be approached from at least three perspectives, and all of them are valid in answering the question.

- I have to give a presentation. Nobody told me I was assessed on presentation skills.

- Nothing in media and cultural studies is free of controversy and conflict.

- There is no one version of media and cultural studies which all undergraduates study.

- Media production degrees are as demanding as all other degree courses at university.

- Media production also means studying theories and concepts.

There are a set of other discoveries:

> Doing media and cultural studies has made me less certain about the media and culture than when I started the degree. But doing

media and cultural studies has made me more critical, more reflective, and more inquisitive. I can go on to do postgraduate study, train in teaching or enter a number of professions and careers.

There are lots of other items which could be listed above. Perhaps the single most important area is the one to do with certainty. At the end of the third year of study, students do know more than when they started in the first year. However, perhaps the qualities that are required for a greater knowledge base are not so much to do with volume or activity. Rather, they are to do with being inquisitive, critical and self-critical, open to the views and perspectives of others, alert to feedback and criticism, aware of how to study, and to make the most of the space and time which undergraduate study permits. The idea of certainty is linked to two other areas which have preoccupied universities: 'truth' and 'knowledge'. Students, academics and all those involved in universities continue to be concerned with knowledge. However, the university's relation to knowledge is one of discovery but also construction. This is also true of the media. Although media industries report events, any two reports about one event suggest that it is not limited to one meaning. Although university degree programmes, then, are concerned with truth, with knowledge and answers to problems, university courses are equally concerned with how a topic is approached, the ways in which the answer is arrived at, and the perspectives and the evidence used in the construction of knowledge. This critical, questioning approach applies across all aspects of media and cultural studies degrees, whether in the form of theories and essays or in the form of media productions such as radio reports, newspaper articles or recorded interviews.

OVERVIEW OF THE BOOK

Part I: Understanding Media and Culture

Part I is divided into two chapters. Chapter 1 considers the questions 'What are the media? What Is media studies?' It provides a short, clear account which outlines key activities, institutions and forms associated with the media and cultural industries, and an outline of the rationale and logic which underpin media studies degrees. Issues of employability, employment and further study will be addressed in relation to the range and type of courses students can study. These issues are also developed in Part III. In keeping with the book's concern to develop and encourage critical questioning and inquiry, however, it will also demonstrate how the study of the media is one of the ways of studying the wider aspects of local and international cultures.

Chapter 2 is concerned with the questions 'What Is Culture? What Is Cultural Studies?' It outlines and discusses key notions of culture and popular culture in terms of *way of life, everydayness, practices* and *texts*. A brief history of the development of the idea of culture will preface a discussion of how culture means more than *Culture* with a capital 'C'. A range of key concerns within cultural studies will be introduced, followed by a discussion of what is involved when thinking about human societies from the perspectives of cultural studies. The section will consider what sorts of careers or postgraduate study routes students can consider in relation to the field of cultural studies.

Part II: Topics, Themes and Debates in Media and Cultural Studies

Part II discusses audiences in media and cultural studies; cultural identities; media representations; visual texts, television and film; cultural production and consumption; newspapers and magazines; popular culture and popular music; subcultures; theories of media; theories of culture. These brief discussions are written in the spirit of inquiry and criticism, encouraging readers to develop their own questions, and to indicate how media and cultural studies degrees intersect with the spheres and concerns which are local and international, and personal and 'Political' with a capital 'P'. Part II provides a structured outline of some of the principal terms, concepts and areas of research in media and cultural studies, topics central to degrees in these fields. However, the emphasis is less on providing an exhaustive discussion and is focused more on encouraging criticism and questions. This section of the book, therefore, does not offer detailed outlines as in standard textbooks. Rather, it provides highlights which allow readers to gain a sense of what is studied on degree programmes, and how to approach the discussion with a critical sense. This section will also be useful for the purposes of essay writing, examinations and extended studies, as well as the closer examination of media and cultural texts, practices and productions. For all of the topics discussed there are suggestions for further reading, and in Part III there are examples of typical essay questions which tie in with the discussions in Part II. Where relevant, production-based activities are also listed for further consideration.

Part III: Study Skills

Part III outlines, discusses and offers advice on the various teaching and learning strategies students will encounter at university. It explains what students can expect in media and cultural studies programmes, and it offers suggestions on writing assignments of various types. Much of the material is structured around worked-through examples based on existing practice in media and cultural studies.

PART I
Understanding Media and Culture

1 WHAT ARE THE MEDIA? WHAT IS MEDIA STUDIES?

INTRODUCTORY OBSERVATIONS

At first sight, it might seem that the questions which entitle the chapter are questions that do not need to be asked. The media are surely anything associated with film, television, radio, magazines and newspapers. Therefore, the mass media have as their objects of study film, television, radio, or simply the media themselves. This kind of answer is sufficiently broad for the opening of a chapter which aims to assist its readers to understand what the media are, and what might be studied on a media studies degree programme. But a degree in media studies will not simply study the media. Nor will a degree programme study the media simply as media. The media – because they intervene in and across the social, political, cultural and personal dimensions of life – are thus central to the understanding of how local and international societies operate in the twenty-first century.

Staying for the moment with questions of the media and media studies, new students will find that the specific focus of degree programmes is never simply the media industries or the output of media such as television or radio. Consider the analysis of television. If television is the object of study, what precisely will be studied? Television drama, news, documentaries, sitcoms and advertisements all count as television output. However, in the programmes listed here, there are some fairly obvious differences. Apart from the fact–fiction divide, it is probably apparent that advertisements are trying to provoke and engage audiences in ways that news programmes and documentaries are not. Nonetheless, news and factual programmes attempt to provoke audiences and draw on dramatic devices more often associated with television dramas. A day spent watching television, for instance, might suggest that all programmes dramatise and embellish what they say and how they say it, at least to some extent. A student, however, would not have the time to spend watching television all day (despite what the popular media say about students!). But a media studies student would be interested in the evidence for and against the claim that all television output is embellished and dramatised. Moreover, media studies would be interested in the methods and approaches deployed in order to ascertain the truth or falsity of the claim. In addition, media analysts and theorists would need at some point to work with audiences. Because all media output has or assumes an audience, then a degree in media studies will be concerned with understanding and interpreting audiences. Any form of media analysis – whether of film, television, radio or other medium – which ignores readers, viewers, listeners and spectators – is an analysis which will remain limited and partial. The terms used in these opening comments, ranging as they do from global and political dimensions of the media to the groups who make and consume the media, make the media an exciting course of study on which to embark. The next sections provide details as to these courses of study and the directions in which media and media studies travel.

WHAT ARE THE MEDIA?

A book of this sort will not provide the complex definitions and arguments that surround what is meant by the media. In many ways, the critical discussion, analysis and assessment of the media in contemporary cultures proves more interesting and exciting than defining an object of study. However, at the beginning of undergraduate study, definitions and frameworks can help in allowing students to arrange their own structures for learning and to establish research agendas fairly quickly. Most media studies programmes will be arranged around modules (see below). These modules, crucial to your programme of study on all media and cultural studies degrees, make assumptions and provide definitions of the media which converge around the following subheadings.

The 'object' of study

The mass media can be understood in relation to

1. media producers;
2. media institutions and organisations;
3. media audiences/users;
4. media output.

Television audiences, for instance, might watch a news programme, a format which, like sitcoms, documentaries or soap operas, is part of the daily output of the television industry. The news is a part of the organisation's (for example, BBC's) output. It will have been put together and produced by BBC personnel – a production team – and will have involved people who edit, report, check sound or provide continuity. Media studies will be concerned with understanding how all these interlocked domains of the media operate in the construction and representation of human cultures.

Media analysis will seek to discuss, examine and assess *all* the components which constitute the media. The more critical the analysis, the more interesting the dynamics of the media and media output can become. The object of study, then, is something which can be described (as above) and it is something which can be analysed. Approached critically and analytically, by students who are interested in asking further questions about the media's power and influence, then media studies is a programme which seeks to understand how the world can be shaped by media industries and practitioners. But because the media are never neutral or free of ideology or underpinning beliefs about how the world should be or could be represented, then media studies will always be interested in asking questions about the analysis of the media and the analysis of the production of media output.

Media analysis/output

In order to comprehend and embark on media analysis, it will be useful at this stage to consider what is meant by media output. This can be understood in relation to almost everything media producers and organisations put together for audiences: advertisements, magazines, newspapers, films, DVDs, television programmes and comics are familiar, everyday examples of media texts. One way of talking about media output is in terms of the written and spoken narratives and stories and the audio-visual sounds and images – the texts in other words – which construct and represent a specific reality at a particular point in history.

To analyse this output is one way of carrying out media analysis. Degree programmes, then, will encourage students in methods of analysis. Perhaps the main point concerning media analysis (examples of which are discussed later in the book) is that the analysis be understood not just in relation to the text (programme, newspaper, magazine), but in the context of the society and history in which the media is produced. Michael Moore's *Fahrenheit 9/11* (2004), for example, is a very vivid illustration of how the relationships between the mass media and society always matter. On the one hand, his film is made in response to a very specific political situation in America's history and, on the other hand, his own deployment of the media (the making of the film) indicates that how the media represent society and history always has to be investigated. Approaches which attend to historical context are vitally important to the ongoing evaluation and appraisal of the media's role in political and social life.

Media analysis/audiences

But media analysis and media analysts must also consider components of the mass media 'outside' the frames of the texts. Audiences, or the readers, listeners and users of texts, not only interpret texts but also use media output and products in the ongoing (re)construction of everyday life. Thus, what audiences have to say about the texts, and what audiences 'do' with output and products, will form a vital part of any media analysis. Without a sense of what the users think of media output, then media analysis remains textual analysis and, whilst important, it limits how the role of the media is understood in contemporary cultures. If we take as our example Moore's film, it will be important to ask questions not simply about the film (for example, its genre, its use of news footage, its use of Moore himself), but about what audiences made of the film (for example, who watched the film, what sense did audiences make of the film).

Media forms, representations and productions

Media studies can also be represented in terms of the containers into which media content is shaped and packaged. Terms such as genre, narrative, style and form can be used to describe this packaged content, with specific terms such as soap opera, documentary, film noir, sci-fi, pulp fiction, house and rap indicating some of the subdivisions which exist in all media categories. The term 'representation' is used to refer to a range of depictions of social life in film, televisual, musical, linguistic and cultural media. 'Representation' is used in media and cultural analysis to denote not simply written, spoken and visual texts (for example, film, TV documentary, photographs) but to refer to arrangements of signs used in order to generate meanings about people or experiences. Media representations, in the sense that they are textual, are composed of signs which generate meanings about culture and people, and which intersect on national and international planes. But it is production teams which make output. Script-writers put together stories and narratives; sound, recording and camera operators ensure output is accessible to audiences; and reporters and interviewers front the programme or are seen and heard when the output is screened, broadcast or aired.

An organisation like the BBC employs staff who include radio producers, assistant producers, commissioning editors and assistants, broadcast journalists, technology assistants, editorial assistants, education advisers, PAs, heads of trans-missions, television journalism trainers, stenographers and caterers. The production staff for a television soap opera will include writers, directors, script editors, story editors, story associates, casting directors, series editors, designer, head of production, executive producers and producers. For films, the following would all contribute to production: directors, pro-duction companies, producers, unit managers, assistants to producers and managers, script and screenplay personnel, camera operators and assistants, gaffers, stills personnel, editors, special effects, art directors, hairstylists, wardrobes staff, titles and graphics specialists, recording engineers, staff involved in sound and sound effects, opticals and music, and actors! It can be seen, then, that students who enter media studies should be prepared for a range of posts. The univer-sity department or careers office will advise students in more detail about the work and employment opportunities once they take up their places to study at university. It should be noted, however, that media studies students also take up jobs in teaching, social work, human resource management, polit-ical and charitable work, PR, journalism and postgraduate study (to do Master's degrees or PhDs).

MEDIA STUDIES AND MEDIA ANALYSIS

How, then, are the industries and activities as vast and as diverse as those associated with the mass media analysed in formal or quantifiable ways? What kinds of questions need to be asked of the media? Are audiences the place to start, or should questions first be asked of the people who make media output? One way of thinking of these questions, and ones which are asked on all media studies degrees, is via a twofold division of quality and quantity. You are reminded that a book of this kind is only offering introductory observations in order to provide a sense of some of the activities on media studies degrees. The two divisions below are ones which, in the second and third year of study, will be put under scrutiny, perhaps even reformulated in more complex ways though, in the first year, they are important building blocks with which to work. Research and dissertation projects in the final year are excellent places to deploy and test out methods of media analysis.

Quantity

Media studies, then, in its investigations of output, audiences, products and industries will ask questions in at least two ways. Sometimes, media analysis is concerned with quantity. Quantitative research will be concerned with questions which ask:

- how much time is spent watching television

- how many programmes of a specific genre are shown on one night or across the duration of a week

- which specific groups of people watch programmes or listen to the radio at specific times during the day

- who uses mobile and digital media technologies

- how have new media, digital media and media technologies influenced social life

- how far are media representations 'representative' of the society which produces and consumes them

- are the mass media neutral in how they put output together

The questions are potentially endless and, from the above list, it can be seen that some questions have a different urgency attached to them than others. Quantitative research is used by all sorts of constituencies and for various, often conflicting, reasons. For some groups, media research assists the aims of marketing and PR. For others, quantitative media research is concerned with analysing the relations between the media and politics, human behaviour and society.

Quality

Qualitative media research is not disconnected from the enumerative analysis of quantity. However, qualitative research is frequently interested in people's relationships to the media, asking questions about how audiences interpret or decode media output and considering how far the media is instrumental (or not) in shaping ideas and behaviour. Although audiences are central to qualitative and quantitative research, qualitative methods will want to understand the interpretations, readings and meanings of media output which audiences make. Terms such as 'audience reception', 'ethnography', 'case study' and 'decoding' are linked to qualitative research. These methods underline a methodology which will draw on structured interviews, participation and participant observations, and focus group interviews in order to understand media messages. Quantitative research will analyse segments of media output, will present its findings in terms of statistical data and will adopt methods which are broadly positivist. The effects, uses, meanings and cultural consumption of media are central concerns of quantitative research. Qualitative research will analyse media messages as a whole and will ask how audiences construct meanings. The media do not cause people to act in a certain way, and thus the questions of qualitative research will focus on the decoding of the media text or message. These issues of quality and quantity are developed in later sections of the book.

MEDIA STUDIES: DEGREE PROGRAMMES

What will you study on the media studies degree? Will research methods be used? Will there be opportunity to train in radio production, television or print journalism? How do theory and practice link up in media studies? Do degree programmes train students to analyse media output? Do degree programmes provide experiences with lead bodies in the industry? Does media studies include film studies? 'Which is the best course for me?'

Degree programmes in media studies (and cultural studies, though this is discussed in the next section) are not uniform in shape or direction. A brief glance at the following titles, however, provides a sense of many of the courses on offer in UK universities: BA (Honours) in Media Studies, Cultural Studies, Communications Studies, Media Production, Media and Cultural Studies, Media and Film Studies, Media and Communications Studies, Film and Video, New Media, Journalism, Media Practice, Photography, Creative Writing, Media with Marketing, English, Sociology, Psychology and other subjects in the humanities and social sciences. The list is probably much longer, but university brochures and websites give a clearer picture of the aims and objectives of the course. Moreover, all degrees in media studies will make references to 'theory' and 'production' or 'practice'. The issues surrounding these terms are discussed later in the book, but at this stage 'production' is being used to refer to those courses which provide 'hands-on' experience (for example, training in sound, radio, television, reporting and so on), and 'theory' is being used to signal those courses which deal with the social and cultural uses and analysis of the media. In reality, theory and production are not terms which are easily separated; media production degrees draw heavily on theory, and media theory degrees draw heavily on traditions and practices in media production. The division below, therefore, serves a definitional and explicatory purpose.

Production-based studies

Media production degrees, which are NOT the opposite of media theory degrees (all degrees are theoretical *and* critical *and* practical to greater or lesser extents), will allow students to gain experience and practice in the processes of media production more than broad-based media studies degrees. The skills acquired in production degrees will relate to advertising, writing for the print media, script writing, editing, audio production and work in sound, video and television, documentary, photography and multimedia applications. In terms of specific modules, it is often the case that options will include visual cultures and photography, communication technologies, cyber cultures, radio production, working in digital media, new medias and various types of research, professional and employment-related projects. Many degree programmes in media production have close links with media companies, and it is worth investigating the kinds of opportunities the course makes available for undergraduates.

Production-based courses are often taught in 'new-sector' universities, in part because the former polytechnics were founded in order to provide training and education in courses of studies not offered in the 'old' or red-brick sector. The new universities have thus been able to establish centres of excellence in specific areas of media production. Many of the new, but also old-sector, universities offer courses and training in media production, media technologies and new media, often with opportunities to gain practical experience in the media industries. Production-based courses do not necessarily exclude modules in media theory and many universities and degree programmes combine a predominantly practical training with opportunities for study and discussion of the critical theories and perspectives used in media analysis. As already underlined, the terms 'theory' and 'production' do not adequately describe how degree programmes are organised, so the division here is solely for explanatory reasons. Most courses provide opportunities for a range of modules, and it needs to known on television as 'Ali G'. Audiences 'know' Ali G rather than Sacha Baron Cohen (the name he was given at birth). Ali G is the identity which is projected on screens and which is written about in the press. But we can also see in the two names an obvious reference to cultural traditions. Linguistically, and in recent British history, the surname 'Cohen' has come to signify a Jewish history, surname and identity, whereas 'Ali' is usually linked to Muslim or Arab cultures. Yet there is nothing 'natural' or essential about an identity. Rather, the names point us to history, tradition and culture. The apparently simple marker of a 'first' name (often referred to as the 'Christian' name in British culture) or surname points in the direction of way of life, history, geographical location, gender and religion.

In order to highlight the multiple components of his and most identities, it might be useful to start with a very brief résumé of Cohen's own biography, even if this is only to demonstrate how personal biography, whilst important, proves of limited use in the understanding of contemporary identities. Popular magazines and internet sites are keen, as with most media 'celebrities', to draw on biography and personal history in order to reveal the truth behind the media identity, to expose something that the media persona conceals. But, when the press and magazines promise to reveal the truth behind the celebrity's identity, the media will always be forced into further constructions of identity, and not revelations. For instance, Cohen was born to a Welsh-Jewish family in 1971. His family observed synagogue customs and festivals and, during his youth, he spent time working as a volunteer for Habonim Dror, a Jewish youth organisation. After attending a public school in Elstree, he studied history as an undergraduate at Cambridge University. But what does this tell us specifically about Cohen, and what does this tell about the different formations which compose British identities?

In his early years doing the comedy circuits, there is no doubting Cohen's indebtedness to his middle-class Jewish background, and any analysis of his performances and comedy would need to make some reference to his biography. But in examining identity constructions, media and cultural studies degrees seek to confront the limited nature of family and child-hood history in the determination of identity. Cohen, then, has to be understood in relation to the media and culture industries, and the generic formats which have enabled the actor to construct convincingly the identities he has done over the last ten years. Although his characters variously critique popular cultures, street cultures, boy gangs and middle-class values, we can see that Cohen's investment in and reliance on these cultures is as great as the critique he appears to conduct against them. To perform the identities he does, Cohen the comedian-mimic necessarily relies on the popular cultures in which these identities are both legible and credible.

Communicating media identities

It has to be recalled that it is the media industry which itself invests in and constructs these identities by means of formats such as comedy, docu-dramas, young people's television and reality television. In many ways, the discourses of psychiatry and psychology regularly (re)construct identities referred to as 'personality disorders'. If there were a fixed category of personality disorder, then it becomes difficult to account for the regular redefinition of the 'disorder' in the diagnostic and statistical registers. Celebrity identities, psychiatric classifications and sexual identities, for example, are bound up with forms of representation and, in the West, the media and culture industries are in part concerned with the constant reproduction of cultural identities which are then packaged into forms and representations in film, television or music.

It was a reliance on forms of representation (drama and comedy) which allowed Cohen to experiment with a number of formats, eventually leading in 1996 to the Paramount Comedy Channel and Cohen's creation of Bruno, the Austrian whose interviews served to satirise the trends and superficialities of Western Europe's fashion industry. We can see how Cohen's own constructions of identities are in part dependent on the media's own constructions (of race, of class and of gender), but we can see how Cohen himself is implicated in the media, someone who reproduces the media identities which simultaneously produce him. Cohen, performing interviewer Bruno, uses the identity of the fictional reporter to comment satirically on contemporary popular culture, even though it is popular culture which enables Cohen to have the identity he does in the media. A brief period in 1997 with Granada's short-lived teenage programme *F2F* led, in 1998, to Cohen's time working for the *11 O'clock Show* (Channel Four). The show's deliberate overdramatisation of news and current affairs, alongside its ironic examination of the culture industry and world of celebrity, paved the way for Cohen's Ali G of 'East Staines Massive' fame, and Borat, the East European reporter and his hilarious investigations of 'British Life'. But the *11 O'clock Show*'s mixture of genres and narratives, and the engagement of hyperbole and hype in its fantastical 'news' stories, provided Cohen with material to explore the construction of identities in the media.

Taking identity seriously

What is interesting about Cohen's work – both his politically controversial material as well as his more obviously hilarious outbursts – is the parodying as well as critical rearticulation of identities associated with genre conventions. Is Cohen being serious or simply satirical? Are Cohen's parodies an attack on identity categories, on the people who embody the identities or the media which exploits them? Should we take his work seriously or not? Identities are tied to race and gender, but is Cohen, and are his characters, racist or sexist? Questions such as these are important because Cohen's reworking of these conventions serves to expose how recent television and associated culture industries exploit narrative and genre forms in terms of the identity of the 'celebrity'. In relation to the sphere of culture and representation, it might be argued that his creations participate in and critique the unrelenting and melodramatic construction of celebrities and celebrity cultures, particularly in television and popular magazines. Yet his programmes also make sense in this domain of the media, relying as they do on the very media-celebrity circuit his work satirises and mocks. Cohen's attempts to expose the unequal social and economic spheres in which the veneration of celebrity *appears* to happen occurs via the media, suggesting that no identities are inside or outside media representation in any straightforward sense. His work, then, highlights how identity is always in the process of being mediated and constructed, so that *who* one is makes sense in relation to *how* one is represented in linguistic and visual ways.

Cohen's and his characters' participation in the media industry serves to reflect the extent to which identity has to be staged, performed and narrated. Without the frameworks of language and discourse – key elements in all media and cultural analysis – then it is difficult to imagine or talk about identity. Programmes such as *Da Ali G Show* and *The Kumars at No 42* show how identity is derivative and intertextual, something made out of elements of other representations, words, images and texts. These programmes draw attention to identity, poke fun at it, rely on an identity in order to speak and be heard, and demonstrate the discomforting significance of identity categories in contemporary cultures. The programmes are examples of a range of recent television output which relies on a multi-textual as much as a multicultural and multi-ethnic history and context. *The Kumars*, for instance, exposes how British culture is not one thing but is itself composite or made from the remnants of others' traditions. Aware of the politics of identity and ethnicity inside and outside the media, and anticipating viewers' awareness of racial and gender stereotypes, both *Da Ali G Show* and *The Kumars* are programmes which go some way to establishing why it is that matters of identity are always much bigger than the individuals who seem to embody the identity in question. But these are shows which draw on a range of cultural stereotypes in order to highlight the composite and hybrid features of all identities.

FURTHER READING

Malik, S. (2002), *Representing Black Britain: Black and Asian Images on Television*, London: Sage.
Woodward, K. (ed.) (1997), *Identity and Difference*, London: Sage.

5   GENRES: TELEVISION AND FILM

GENRE

Have you ever watched a popular television series or film and, after a short period of time, been able to predict what would happen? Crime dramas, sitcoms, soap operas, classic Westerns, thrillers and romances are genres which allow, and in many ways encourage, audiences to speculate about the plot and the characters, with some reliability. Soap operas come to a provisional 'conclusion' after each episode, leaving audiences with a dilemma or conflict, and encouraging viewers to guess what or who comes next in the plot. Recent British soaps have invited audiences to nominate the hero's bride, and in the case of the UK's longest-running television soap, *Coronation Street*, a national newspaper campaign was mounted to ensure a character's release from prison (the case itself also being raised in a House of Commons debate at Prime Minister's Questions).

Why all this fuss over dramas and genres often labelled 'low quality', and which are frequently dismissed on grounds of their formulaic nature? It's possible to miss the opening minutes of a popular genre but still manage to follow most, if not all, of the episode. In the case of popular film, actors and storylines are packaged according to criteria which will ensure fairly short-term popularity and sales. Actors' lives are dissected on television talk shows, and popular magazines invite audiences to share a 'day in the life of' the celebrity.

Films and television dramas are often described and defined in terms of *genre*. The term is one which indicates that texts are (and will be) classified in certain ways and not others. The classic Western, for instance, can be divided into sixteen narrative functions, and can be analysed in terms of the forces who are on the 'inside' of the society which the Western constructs, and those who are on the 'outside'. To speak of a text's genre is to describe its specific features or shape. Dramas, for instance, might be comic or romantic in form, and films might be thrillers or romantic comedies. As soon as a text's genre is known, then certain predictions can be made about what will happen, to whom, when and why.

In classic film noir, certain claims can be made about the genre's women characters; in television soap operas, certain predictions can be made about the scriptwriters' plotting of births, deaths, murders, marriages and divorces; and 1950s Westerns will invariably present the pioneer and 'his' family in heroic terms. Recent teenage gothic dramas on television (for example, *Buffy*) and romantic comedies (for example, films such as *Bridget Jones' Diary*), can be defined in terms of the specific characteristics of each text and the impact the genre will have on respective audiences. Genre, then, serves the purpose of definition and it allows texts to be classified according to conventions of characterisation, plot and narrative.

Yet genre definitions (for example, gangster films, horror films and more complexly film noir) raise more problems than they solve. We can understand their problematic status in relation to Hollywood, film and the cinema. No genre can be easily isolated from the society and the economy from which it emerged. Hollywood narratives, then, are as much linked to notions of the 'American dream' as they are connected to technology and innovation in film and production practices. Nor do Hollywood narratives and film genres operate outside an ideology which serves to affirm the values of a conservative social order centred around the family and marriage. Yet Hollywood narratives and popular film genres do not simply reflect this ideology. Exceptions to the rule suggest that narrative itself can undermine the very values which the narrative apparently seeks to instate. But popular genres also make money, and can more or less guarantee huge sales inside and outside the cinema.

CONFLICT MODELS OF FILM AND TELEVISION

A degree course in media and cultural studies which examines film media and film cultures will surely examine the above points in detail, but most of the debates and politics surrounding popular film or television will at some point consider details of genre and narrative. One of the most common ways of beginning to look at dramatic and filmic texts is in relation to a *balance–conflict–resolution* model. Television dramas and popular films are of course far more complex than is being suggested here, a complexity which undergraduate-degree programmes will want to explore in greater detail. However, it can be seen that film and television texts, whether popular or whether 'canonical', have to be constructed in certain ways. In film or television genres:

1. Stories will be told from a particular angle.

2. Action of some kind will occur.

3. A sense of time and place will be provided.

4. Characters will generate action.

5. A sense of movement through time, whether linear or not, will become apparent.

6. Action will begin and end.

7. Assumptions are made about implied readers or viewers and actual readers and viewers.

In all genres, a sense of equilibrium or balance will be disturbed by some form of conflict. However, the conflict (no matter how minor) is pivotal in genre and narrative constructions in that it is that which propels the movement of the story. Thrillers or police dramas (for example, *Inspector Morse*, *Prime Suspect*, *The X-Files*) are good examples of how the balance of a particular state of affairs is shattered by conflict or mystery, but audiences know that some resolution or restored balance will come about before the narrative concludes. A media and cultural studies degree will be important in this ongoing analysis and understanding of alternative cinema and drama, although, in the early stages of study, popular genres can be understood schematically on the basis of the following 'conflict–resolution' model:

Stage 1. *Preliminary stages*, which can occur in a range of formats, will: (1) introduce characters; (2) establish a location and setting; (3) construe, not necessarily in this order, events and circumstances, motives and intentions, particular states of affairs; and (4) establish key actions or initiate key events.

Stage 2. *Intermediary stages*, whose constituent parts will overlap with each other as well as with the beginnings and ends of the other stages, will: (1) begin to establish systems of identification within the drama and with audiences; (2) establish character aims and objectives in some detail; (3) position principal characters in relation to key emotional and intellectual domains; (4) construct a web of complications, confusions, perplexities and disconnections; and (5) allude to resolution, solution and connection.

Stage 3. *Developmental and post-intermediary stages* will draw heavily on items in Stage 2 above. However, (1) systems of identification will be intensified or seriously questioned; (2) character aims and objectives will be either affirmed or called into doubt; (3) characters may be repositioned; (4) complications, confusions and perplexities will be provisionally augmented or provisionally diminished; and (5) allusions to resolution may be made more obviously or continue to remain with some sense of indirection or inconclusiveness.

Stage 4. *Outcomes* may: (1) disappoint or surprise viewers; (2) imply viewers were always in a place of knowledge and knew outcomes from the start; (3) allow for outcomes to frustrate happy endings; and (4) establish (provisional) resolution and establish an end or a new departure.

GENRE: HISTORIES AND INDUSTRIES

In many ways, these accounts of film and television genres, and of contemporary popular cultures in general, are usefully understood in the historical context of, first, industrialisation and, secondly, mass production. Genres, star systems and interest in celebrities are also major features of nineteenth-century popular cultures. The industrial revolution brought an economic wealth to Britain and Western Europe, and some of this wealth served to lay the foundations of urban popular cultures. Places of entertainment and public singing did not emerge by chance in the nineteenth century. Rather, they were tied to increases in population, increased urbanisation and the rise of a cultural domain which complemented in a complex way (and at times resisted) the economic domain of work and labour. There is much evidence to suggest that nineteenth-century melodrama, music hall and the early days of the cinema were also celebrated and denigrated in ways that the genres of popular culture are today. The star system emerged at the end of the nineteenth century, and celebrity status – as today – depended a great deal on the favours or otherwise of impresarios, audiences and the press.

Yet the notion of genre predates nineteenth-century popular cultures by quite some time. Opera can be classified in terms of genre, and the plays of the Elizabethan and Jacobean periods are often discussed in terms of their fulfilment (or not) of genre categories and expectations associated with tragedy or comedy. Historically, it was literary output that was first grouped under the three key formal headings which divided drama, poetry and prose. Of course, within these broad arrangements, further subdivisions existed. Classical Greek drama, for instance, is described and defined as comic or tragic. Tragedy and comedy follow specific paths and pursue different aims. In the work of Aristotle, one of the first exponents of drama, the tragic plot is designed to arouse pity and fear, leading audiences to experience a catharsis or cleansing. More commonly today, popular cultural texts are listed and promoted as thrillers or sitcoms, though, within these categories, further subdivisions proliferate: teen soaps (*Hollyoaks*), anicoms (*The Simpsons*), police psychological thrillers (*Cracker*) and so on. In film studies, the classifications include gangster films, film noir, horror films and Westerns. Within these classifications, further subdivisions might include teenage horror, British Hammer horror, 'slasher' films and psychological horrors. But the film classifications also make sense in the context of later industrial change and the strengthening of capitalist economic expansion. Thus, Hollywood is referred to as a 'system' whose operations, including the studio system, are directly linked to specific working practices. A media and cultural studies degree programme, then, will not simply be interested in the analysis of genre, but in the wider history in which the genre is made intelligible.

FANTASY FICTIONS

In many ways, the number of subgenres and hybrid versions of genres (for example, docusoap, docudrama) suggests that genre boundaries may no longer serve as useful ways of describing popular cultural forms with any reliability. Understood within the broader culture, however, it can be seen that genres also serve as ways of categorising experience and of describing how people live in relation to others. Genres, and fictions more generally, are one of the principal means of making sense of human experience. Genres allow the complexity and enormity of social life to be provisionally managed, observed and understood. Films and television dramas do not directly reflect or mirror an actual or real world in any straightforward sense so much as they construct a reality.

These fictional representations allow the mundane realities of everyday life to be examined and criticised. Fiction is never simply 'fiction' or fantasy, so much as it is made intelligible in the contexts of its uses. However, do the popular genres screened in cinemas or on television represent a cultural reality with which you are familiar? Is this cultural reality one which captures, represents, constructs or distorts the reality? Are groups left out of the representation, and why? These kinds of questions will be encouraged on media and cultural studies degree programmes, and should be embraced as important parts of the course, especially in seminars or as prompts for essays.

The current popularity of garden makeover programmes, DIY and cookery shows is partly a reflection of a television channel's reliance on viewing figures and audience share (and thus revenue). Television and film make sense in the wider settings of capitalist economies. But capitalism itself relies on fantasies: of wealth, individual freedom and of being able to realise a dream as a result of hard work. Similarly, Western television output also operates on the basis of fantasy and desire. In that sense, holiday and travel programmes, but particularly television output structured around discourses of domestic bliss (for example, via representations of a second or early-retirement home) serve a utopian function. The programme constructs a fantasy of escape, contentment and (apparent) freedom. But these fantasies of escape, which are not restricted by any means to the popular genres of recent television, promise an ideal which makes sense in terms of the economic and social realities of lived experience outside the genre. The programmes posit a reality, but does the fantasy truthfully reflect the lived experiences of audiences?

A closer examination of the history of television genres suggests that the idealisation of the home and the family, via cookery and DIY programmes, has always been part of television's scheduling. In today's output, spectacular garden improvements, impressive loft conversions and images of perfect living spaces are part of a utopian, pastoral and romantic legacy which contemporary television exploits in the deregulated world of television programming. But it is to be stressed that this is a legacy which predates television and film. Fine art and paintings, in their appropriation of the same genres and conventions, are measured by different standards to the ones which are imposed on popular genres and popular output. It is thus perhaps questions of the functions and uses of cultural capital, rather than the object of culture, which will be of ongoing concern to debate in cultural studies.

INSIDE AND OUTSIDE GENRES

All cultural output – that which is mass-produced as well as that which is 'authored' – is constructed in relation to formulas. The formulas, in that all culture can be understood in relation to structures and conventions, are by no means limited to popular genres. 'High culture', or Culture with a capital 'C', is itself framed according to formulaic and often quite rigid considerations. Television scheduling, though far less obviously structured than it was in the 'golden age' of television in the 1970s, is put together in relation to formulas, expectations and audience viewing habits. Yet popular film is no less able to shock audiences than the work of avant-garde directors or experimental output. Hitchcock's output, for instance, can be read in terms of popular culture, in terms of the auteur or author tradition, in relation to American studies, or in relation to the conflicting expectations of structuralist, feminist or queer critique. Moreover, all cultural output is regulated at least to some extent, whether this is 'high culture' or film and television. British television exists partly in relation to Acts of parliament, public policies and government regulations. Similarly film is subject to censorship and control.

Perhaps media and cultural studies degrees, then, are well placed in the analysis of output which will be measured not just in terms of its meaning or impact, but in relation to the social structures, moral conventions, state regulations and ideologies which surround any text or practice. Media and cultural studies degrees are interested in all these areas with the aim of providing a detailed and full account of how mass media and cultures function in a given society.

FURTHER READING

Creeber, G. (ed.) (2001), *The Television Genre Book*, London: BFI.
Thornham, S. and Purvis, T. (2005), *Television Drama: Theories and Identities*, Basingstoke: Palgrave Macmillan.

6 AUDIENCES IN MEDIA AND CULTURAL STUDIES

AUDIENCES AND MEDIA OUTPUT

How important are audiences in media and cultural studies? Is it possible to have media output for which there is no audience? Who determines what audiences do with messages? Is the message ultimately more important than the audiences which receive the message? These sorts of questions will be raised with some frequency in media and cultural studies degrees. Moreover, modules specifically interested in audience studies are increasingly listed in undergraduate programme guides in media studies. An audience research project, for instance, is an interesting and valuable way of concluding a degree in media or cultural studies. Audience research involves working in quantitative and qualitative terms, allowing students to measure statistically readership or ratings, and then to assess the meanings which audiences attach to particular texts or activities.

In cultural studies, and especially the study of cultural consumption and meaning, the audience is a key element in any form of analysis. The analysis of texts and cultural products is as much concerned with the recording and analysis of what audiences say about the uses and meanings of these texts as it is the texts themselves. But audiences have an economic and financial role as much as they function to make texts mean one thing and not another. 'Audience ratings' and 'audience shares' are not simply terms used to measure audience numbers. They can indicate who is watching which programme at a particular time. Knowing how many people watch a programme is important for PR and advertising companies, political parties and social researchers. Ratings and shares have become important in the increasingly deregulated and privatised world of media production, where audiences are also consumers and markets. But audiences are also people who self-identify in other ways and who attempt to resist the labels which market-led models of media consumption impose on audiences.

All media output, then, is understood in relation to audiences. And all audiences are defined in terms of watching, listening to, or reading media *products* (television programme, radio broadcast or CD, or newspaper). On the one hand, media output is produced in order to make money, tied as all the media are to the economic and financial constraints of national and global markets. On the other hand, media output is made in relation to the audience's demand for this output. Local newspapers, for example, frequently have a base in the town or region of the newspaper's circulation. It is not the case that the local press is free of the constraints of bigger companies and organisations. While they do not have the financial independence that is often assumed, local newspapers nonetheless are identified in terms of the reciprocal relationships they have with their readers and particular 'communities' (however imagined). This notion of the audience – one which is founded on the twofold processes of production (going to press) and consumption (reading the paper) – is a fairly straightforward model of how audiences can be conceived.

AUDIENCES AND LOCAL NEWSPAPERS

The local newspaper is a useful starting point for understanding some of the details of audiences and producers, and of seeing how the media product establishes its relationship with its readers. A brief summary of this dynamic serves to introduce a number of the arguments that will surely be raised in the first year of a media and cultural studies degree programme.

1. Local newspapers have *actual* readers who, whether living in the region or the town, will buy the newspaper on the basis of its connection with the reporting of local issues. Here, the newspaper acts as point of identification, both

for the region as geographical and cultural space, as well as the people who live in the region.

2. Newspapers also have readers who are imagined or *implied* via editorial columns or letters to the editor. For instance, editorials offer a specific comment or insight and, having adopted a position in relation to a local issue or event, will allow the (implied) reader to identify with the editorial comments being made.

3. Local newspapers also address audiences on the basis of difference. The newspaper's very 'localness' is a key factor in establishing its identity as different from the national press and thus in identifying its readers. And, within the newspaper itself, local news and issues are frequently reported in terms of specific geographical locations within the region, or on the basis of social differences (children's section, holiday pages, cultural life of the city or region). In other words, the newspaper audience has a single identity (all the readers constitute the audience at any one point) and a plural identity (the disparate groups and identities serve to compose the audience).

4. Letters pages, the organising of local campaigns via the newspaper, details of local politics, readers' reactions to this via short reports and readers' articles and columns mean that the audience, in imaginary and actual ways, is able to offer its own feedback to the newspaper.

5. Advertisers use the local press in order, in part, to generate consumer needs but also to encourage audiences to buy one product above another. However, advertising is vital to the survival of the newspaper, and the advertising companies can be considered as audiences on which the newspaper relies for an important part of its income.

CONFLICTING AUDIENCES

Audiences on the above model are groups of people who are positioned at the reception-end of message production. But the model outlined is also one which assumes a public role for the newspaper (to serve its communities of readers) and a public sphere in which the newspaper is received and read. The audience on this model is not only part of a public sphere but also has a role to play in this sphere, and the media has a public duty to serve the people. The audience is in a position to comment on the accuracy and effectiveness of the media's role in society. The audience has, then, a very public duty: it comments on and interprets the media messages and, as a result, provides feedback to the producers. Terms such as listeners, readers, viewers and spectators denote some of the activities of audiences. Historically, audiences have had a public role. We can see in the example of the newspaper that an audience is that group of people who not only receive a message and take from it some form of pleasure, entertainment or information, but also provide feedback to the press. However, audiences, as noted, are also markets and consumers, people who use the cultural products and services of what are ultimately big media businesses. In an increasingly deregulated public sphere, then, the public role of audiences will need to be reimagined in relation to the world of the new media. The internet, for instance, is fast becoming an alternative medium. The public sphere which the internet brings together is one which is useful in the mobilisation of groups who are also able to challenge the power of the press, which publishing and advertising industries have in dominating the kinds of media messages that are produced and transmitted.

QUESTIONING AUDIENCES

These points may seem straightforward enough, but on media and cultural studies degrees it will be important to examine further the perceptions and social composition of the audience. If audiences receive information and then interpret this information, then surely the task of media and cultural analysis will be concerned with how texts generate the meanings they do amongst audiences. Knowing what audiences do with texts, or what audiences think, is also an activity which has an ethics attached to it. Questions regarding the motivations of the research project, and its respective researchers, are thus of some importance. It is to be underlined that market research, ethnographic studies and content analysis are not without their own agendas.

However, if the audience is the market, then the meanings and interpretations audiences give to texts will matter far less than how to get customers to buy and consume the product. If the aim is to sell something, why would content matter? But if content does not matter, then what is being sold? The terms used to define the audience, and the questions which surround the function of audiences, hopefully begin to suggest that the media are not free of ideology. The media are not external or objective to culture and society, but help to shape the society's values and belief systems. Often the press has been in a position to determine what people should think, and has instructed readers on 'right' action ('vote this way and not that', 'support this cause', 'this is what happened'). It is easy to see how 'propaganda models' of the media (see later discussions) might want to remind audiences and critics alike that television and print-based news reports function in powerful and determining ways in the formation of public opinion. Election campaigns rely on the mass media to deliver messages, and so it is via the media that the attempt to position audiences (voters) in supportive rather than antagonistic ways actually occurs. To refer to people as the 'audience' rather than as 'consumers', or to refer to people as 'subjects' as opposed to 'individuals', begins to indicate that names and labels in media and cultural studies should always be critically scrutinised and not taken for granted. If 'meanings' (of media output, of aims and intentions of media producers and the meanings audiences make) are never neutral, neither are the terms for the people at the receiving end of media representations.

POSITIONING AUDIENCES

We can gain an initial sense of the inter-operations of messages and producers, and audiences and users, in relation to the framework below. The left-hand column highlights how audiences interpret and actively choose to watch (or not) a particular television programme (or read a newspaper). The right-hand column indicates how far audiences are constrained by structures. In the right-hand column, audiences do not have the ability to self-determine in the ways that 'active audience theories' (associated with the left-hand column) might imply. Rather than audiences receiving and then positioning the text, the right-hand column lists terms which underline how audiences are shaped by discourse.

Audiences, actions and agency	Audiences and structures
Self-determination	Predetermination
Activity	Passivity
Agency and action	Structure and discourse
Choice	Social and cultural constraint
Independent	Dependent

Of course, models such as these can be reductive, and in all studies they should not be used to oversimplify what is a complex operation. In many ways, the model itself, and the terms which appear to separate activity and passivity neatly, will be called into question and deconstructed on media and cultural studies degrees. However, the terms are used because they typify the kind of language which will be encountered in seminar discussions and lectures in the first year of study. They are also terms which are worth pursuing further, especially in relation to their usage in other topics in media studies (for example, social constructionism, cultural production and consumption, subcultures).

In many ways, the points raised about newspapers and readers are made in the spirit of active audience theory (the left-hand column). Ethnographic approaches to audience measurement have variously supported this model in findings and research exercises. However, a number of issues can be raised which begin to complicate the model.

1. Ethnography is a methodology, and brings with it some of the assumptions of a 'realist' theory of knowledge. Realist methodologies have often assumed that social research *discovers* rather than *constructs* a 'real' world. (Degree programmes will seek to enlarge and develop the argument summarised here.)

2. Ethnography itself is forced to use the devices associated with literary and figurative writing, and so the terms of ethnographic research will always to some extent determine the object. Ethnographic research cannot accurately reflect or represent an 'objective' reality but always reports others' representations of experiences of reality.

3. More generally, active audience studies might consider how far the public sphere is not so much a space inhabited by audiences as it is something which discourses and texts construct for audiences. Processes are always indirect in the construction of meaning, and constraints govern and structure producers as much as audiences. This is not to suggest that the mass media determine meanings more than audiences or vice versa, but it is to suggest that a media representation has first to be constructed for it to be interpreted by media audiences.

PROPAGANDA MODELS OF MESSAGES AND AUDIENCES

It is the media's power in the constructing and shaping of the news message that interests 'propaganda-model' theorists

such as Noam Chomsky. Understanding audiences in relation to the propaganda model reveals the ways in which
media messages are filtered according to particular sets of
ideologies and conventions. A propaganda model does not
focus initially on the media, on messages or on audiences but
rather considers the social and economic situations in which
audiences receive messages. In the work of critics such as
Chomsky, it is questions of wealth and power which are
primary in any understanding of media output and the audience. The vested interests of the mass media, in Chomsky's
view, are often entangled with capitalism's profit motives, so
that it is the requirement to increase profit margins which
shapes what audiences see. In order to perceive social and
political relations in one way and not another, the media
has to monitor its own output carefully, particularly what is
presented as 'the news'. The media is 'big business' in a capitalist economy. And because of its involvements with other
major global business, it is forced to *filter* the news. This
filtering effectively marginalises people and groups who
call the news into doubt. This makes it easier for governments, but particularly private enterprise, to determine news
content. Whilst audiences may be in a position to interpret
or decode the news, the fact that the news is filtered from
the start means that any decoding is always limited by prior
filtering.

The news is packaged and managed, says Chomsky, in ways
that don't totally dupe audiences, but in ways that never fully
allow audiences access to the truth of the facts of the case. As
a result, audience interpretation is impaired because filtering
also ensures that the premises by which the news might be
decoded are determined in advance. Certain discourses are
established as more reliable than others, and these discourses
serve only to define and limit any sense of newsworthiness.
Alternative media, therefore, will always find it difficult to
compete, partly because of the dominant messages conveyed
by global news operations and partly because the alternative
media have to convince audiences that there might, in fact, be
an alternative way for audiences to be provided with 'news'.

The media, contends Chomsky, is able to stand outside democratic accountability, dominated as the media is by a small elite who can marginalise dissident voices. News is filtered (for example, via the pressure from advertisers, global corporations and governments) in ways that call into doubt not so much the reporters or people who work in the media, but the claims to objectivity that media organisations make on grounds of 'professional news values'. For instance, in considering the newsworthiness of a particular national government's interventions in global affairs (for example, in 'illegal' wars), the media, according to the propaganda model, are never fully enabled to report what they think are the facts of the case. Nor do they have the freedom to cast doubt on the state's action. Chomsky suggests that while events and stories are reported in the news, audiences can only decode an agenda which is manoeuvred in advance of the media's own construction and representation of a particular action. Chomsky suggests that an analysis of the media and audiences must first inquire into how the media might be imagined as if outside the constraints and filters which determine what will be reported in the first instance.

We can see, then, that the study of audiences in media and cultural studies encourages interesting, lively and important debates. Whichever model of the audience is adopted for purposes of analysis, the analysis will at some point always focus on the constraints or otherwise which position audiences in one way and not another. Yet in being positioned by media output, audiences nonetheless seem able to produce meanings which run against the grain of the texts which would seek to fix the audience and determine its behaviour.

FURTHER READING

Abercrombie, N. and Longhirst, B. (1998), *Audiences: A Sociological Theory of Performance and Imagination*, London: Sage.
Morley, D. (1980), *The 'Nationwide' Audience*, London: BFI.

USEFUL INTERNET RESOURCES

http://web.mit.edu/linguistics/www/chomsky.home.html
http://www.chomsky.info/

7 POPULAR CULTURES

IS POPULAR CULTURE 'CULTURE'?

Some critics would say a very resounding and exclamatory 'Yes!' to this question. Others would say that the question does not need to be asked. And some critics and commentators would say a very definite and resounding 'No!' This 'no' is especially definite when popular culture is linked to, or made to mean, 'mass culture'. But if culture, using Williams's very broad definition means 'way of life', then there is no immediate reason why popular culture is no more or no less culture than what some critics would refer to as 'high' culture. But terms such as 'commercial culture', 'consumer culture', 'postmodern culture', 'mass culture', and 'popular culture' are often paired with an imaginary or ideal 'Culture' (with a capital 'C'), where one way of life, that of 'Culture', is figured in better terms than others. Of course the problem which attends these claims is always one which impacts on the people whose culture is being described or examined.

Perhaps at this stage we can agree that popular culture is culture (a way of life) as much as any other 'culture'. But perhaps we can also agree that the contentions and disagreements which surround the debate point to the importance of its discussion and analysis in the university. The analysis of popular culture has increasingly become a field of study at undergraduate and postgraduate level in its own right. However, it remains one of the most interesting and one of the most controversial areas in cultural studies degrees. Popular culture study is also popular with students; and its study encompasses fields such as popular music, youth cultures, magazines and reading behaviour, fashion and style, subcultures, club cultures and activities and practices that might be considered well liked, undertaken by many or mass produced for mass markets.

SERIOUS CULTURAL STUDIES

Perhaps one of the issues that makes popular culture study contentious is that it is often imagined – inside and outside academic institutions – that anyone who studies culture in its popular expressions and manifestations could not really be a serious student or critical scholar. And because popular culture study is linked to the study of the mass media and mass production, then it is often imagined that mass output can't be differentiated in the ways that the study of 'Culture' can be. 'Culture' has historically been privileged as aesthetically refined and civilising, and popular culture has been understood as common, collective and formulaic. However, it needs to be made clear that popular culture is worth studying, it is worth studying seriously, and it is seriously useful in terms of the insights it provides into society, history and politics. However, so-called 'Culture' with a capital 'C' is also worth studying seriously, and for the same reasons. So where do the 'problems' about popular culture lie?

It is in the description 'popular' that some of the controversy lies. Popular culture is not to be confused with, but nor is it disconnected from, mass culture, folk culture and working-class culture. Its associations with 'mass culture' have linked popular culture to notions of mass deception, the belief that popular mass culture keeps people uncritically happy and therefore blind to life's social and political realities. There is sufficient evidence to suggest that popular cultural texts do not impact in direct or unequivocal ways on how people lead their lives in culture. But mass culture and popular culture, because they are often described solely in terms of the formulaic and the manufactured, are thought to be less authentic and less civilising than high culture.

Yet the range of meanings and nuances attached to 'popular culture' is vast. Popular culture can also mean – as Raymond

Williams suggests – common or low or base. He also defines how popular can mean 'widely favoured' and 'well liked'. Popular can additionally mean 'courting the favour of the people by undue practices', though it might finally mean a culture which was defined as popular, truly a culture of the people, but a culture not defined by the people. Williams also identifies terms such as popular literature, popular press, popular journalism, popular entertainment, popular song and popular art, the last two of which became known as pop songs and pop art. By shortening the word 'popular' to 'pop', Williams suggests the word seems lively and informal, but such informality might serve to trivialise a way of life which is far from inconsequential.

FORMULAS FOR CULTURE

A number of theoretical perspectives is used in the analysis of popular culture and particularly in relation to the study of popular music and popular fiction. These perspectives allow popular culture to be viewed in a certain light and not others. Some theories see culture and popular culture in terms of their relation to the economy. It is the economy which, in the last analysis, dominates how people in society are required, because of income and wealth, to live in one particular way and not another. In some perspectives, popular culture, and popular music in particular, are thought to replicate the monotony of labour in the factory or place of work. If work in mass, automated society is carried out in conditions which require workers to repeat the same task day after day without any need for thought or creativity, so popular music is manufactured according to formulas which do not require musicians or listeners to engage critically or constructively. The music is mass produced, manufactured for audiences whose discernment is such that the music, like the society which produced it, is not called into question. On this reading, popular culture acts as a sedative, deadening cognitive and critical faculties.

love, togetherness, passion or desire; marriage or heterosexual relations are usually idealised; the introduction of the heroine and hero makes way for conflict but ultimate resolution; and the blurb on the back makes clear the novel's romance, intrigue and potential for both readers' and characters' happiness.

It is more than likely that the name of the author on the front cover of a popular romance novel is not the actual name of the author. The extract provided above is written according to a formula and in line with the conventions adopted in all popular romance fiction. In that sense, why would the author matter? Proposals to publishers are required to follow a specific series of guidelines for the writing of the romance, and accompanying notes instruct writers in the writing of the finer details of romantic conflict.

CRITICISMS OF POPULAR CULTURES

Popular music, for similar reasons to Mills and Boon fictions, is often singled out by critics for its formulaic qualities. Criticism of popular culture, especially music and fiction, begins in the early twentieth century and is informed by various critical traditions. Some attack popular music and fiction on moral grounds. Unlike great works of literature and art, popular fiction does not require its readers, it is argued, to think beyond the 'here and now' of the plot. For other theorists, popular music is associated with mass culture and – more worrying still for some critics – America and Americanisation. The words which are used to describe popular music include 'standardised', 'one-dimensional', 'inauthentic', and 'manufactured'. It is also music which requires passive listeners who, acting in conformity with the song, similarly act in conformity with the demands of the economic and social system which produced such inactive listening.

Popular music and popular-music performers are manufactured in the same way that brands and material products are throughout the rest of the economy. Standard formats are required, and so music is produced according to fairly specific guidelines. As a result, popular music is often thought to lack variation and melody. Lyrics, moreover, are often structured around songs with only two or three verses, a chorus and a bridge. Thirty-two-bar sequences, with frequently repeated refrains and catchphrases, serve to 'hook' audiences into the mechanistic process reproduced in the music. Whilst production processes during the twentieth century became more and more sophisticated, popular music, it is often argued, is more and more simple. And it is thought to satisfy a lack in an uncritical audience. But audiences who consume popular music are thought to be inattentive and distracted. By affirming popular music's standardised patterns, the audience are both emotively and rhythmically obedient.

As suggested, shows such as BBC's *Fame Academy* and ITV's *Pop-Idol* rely on the standardised formulas of contemporary popular music and entertainment in order to attract audiences and thus increase market (audience) shares. The individual contestant's image, sound, looks and 'personality' are constructed and understood in relation to the iconic status of a popular music celebrity whose own (manufactured) image and work sets the standard for the show's contestants. But the cult of the personality is established, and it is another way for the programme to attract audiences: the show, like the celebrity, speaks to 'you'.

POPULAR BRANDS

Much of popular culture is produced in relation to cultural and media formulas, and these formulas are not limited to romances for women or popular music. They pervade television and are marketed as follows (at the time of writing):

Monday: BBC1, 5.35 p.m., *Neighbours*.

Monday: ITV1, 7.30 p.m., *Coronation Street*.

Monday: BBC1, 8.00 p.m., *Eastenders*.

Monday: BBC1, 10.00 p.m., *News*.

Saturdays on BBC1, after 12.00 midday, are invariably given over to sports programmes; and Saturdays on ITV1 and BBC1 before 12.00 midday are devoted to children's programmes. Outside the time slots and programme names, audiences can rely on the fictional or actual names of people associated with what is very popular output. Certain names, for instance, are associated with very popular light entertainment; other names will signify a particular television soap opera; and yet other names are associated with early morning news, breakfast shows, chat shows or news bulletins. In the case of popular television, audiences know what to expect regardless of the inflections and twists which the particular episode or programme might take.

However, a range of theoretical and empirical studies has rightly cautioned against the uncritical dismissal of popular culture, both in terms of structures and in terms of readers and audiences more generally. Moreover, these studies have highlighted that critique of popular culture is often predicated on a deficit model: popular culture is lacking whereas as 'Culture' is not. But the deficit model is difficult to sustain. Many ethnographic studies have shown how people use popular cultural texts in reactionary, oppositional and enriching ways. Popular cultural texts can seem to affirm the status quo, yet they can equally provide the very material by which to undermine and question the established order. If it is textual properties which are being examined, then there is no final measure which allows one cultural text to be deemed more valuable than others. Texts, in other words, say and do different things at the same time as generating different expectations. Ethnographic studies additionally suggest that it is how texts are used by audiences, and how the meanings are manipulated by readers or listeners, which generate potentially more interesting sites of research. Feminist studies of readings and cultural studies of the media, especially television, suggest that the selection, interpretation and appropriation of texts is always greater than the seemingly transparent intention of the authors or producers.

A short history of branding

However, the production and consumption of popular romance paperbacks, alongside many popular television shows, are in part connected to the changes in industrial production which occurred during the twentieth century. The romance genre itself predates the television and the Mills and Boon versions by quite a few centuries. Indeed, despite the criticisms to which popular cultures are subjected, none of the generic formulas are wholly new. From the late nineteenth century, mass production, alongside the increasing stress which was placed on the division of labour, specialisation and consumption impacted on notions of good taste, literary quality and culture. Some critics and commentators, from the eighteenth century onwards, have always expressed concern about the practices and manifestations of popular culture. In that sense, there is nothing new about the 'complaints' tradition. But the theoretical, historical and empirical evidence regularly serves to complicate how popular fiction or music might be understood.

First, much cultural output is written in relation to forms, formats and conventions. Comedy, tragedy and romance predate popular twentieth-century material by some considerable time, though it is rare for earlier works to be subjected to the kinds of criticism which popular output has been over the last fifty years. Secondly, much eighteenth-century popular culture, for example, though produced in relation to formulae, is today considered 'high' culture. History surveys of the period 1700–1820 show two distinct cultures in Britain. One version surely reflects the learned and formal culture of the grammar schools, universities and the educated classes; and the other version, with its links to market places and sites of common assembly, reflects the popular culture of the period. But both are necessary in the formation of each culture, and both are necessary in the analysis of the period under scrutiny. The two cultures, then, are interrelated in a complex way and operate on each other in the formation of the wider, more plural eighteenth-century culture. But even within these broad divisions of educated culture and popular culture, there is evidence to suggest much finer divisions and separations, so that, within the former culture, sharp distinctions of taste serve to differentiate one particular aesthetic from another. Apart from the differential distribution of cultural products across different social groups, yet further refinements can be made when consideration is given to the uses and multiple appropriations of cultural forms and artefacts.

Cultural distinctions

Much of the historical and intellectual legacy which has informed the distinctions between high (or sometimes 'official') and popular culture is informed by the increasingly market- and commercial-led distinctions of the eighteenth century. When cultural goods and artefacts can be bought, sold and exchanged for money, then the more expensive the goods, the more cultural taste is endowed with the purchase and the purchaser. 'Taste' (what people judge as good or bad in culture) increasingly became a marker of social differentiation, allowing distinctions to be made not just on grounds of social class, but on how an individual in the class was able to talk about 'culture'. But it is important to note that what, in the eighteenth century, the educated might have referred to as 'vulgar' or 'low' culture is today referred to as 'popular' culture; but it is also a culture whose importance to the understanding of the period cannot be underestimated. Similar distinctions are seen to mark the nineteenth century as well. Whilst the free municipal galleries, libraries and public reading rooms of the late nineteenth century increased working-class access to cultural output and literacy, so those with wealth and income maintained cultural distinctions by travelling to the galleries, exhibitions and sites of archaeological merit in Italy, France, Greece and Spain. In other words, in whichever way the cultural goods of a period are judged, the fact of the judgement perhaps says as much about the culture and its subjects more than the actual goods themselves.

Research into what audiences do with cultural products also suggests that the distinctions between high culture and popular culture continue to inform how 'postmodern' cultures are understood today. On the one hand, popular culture has been seen as something which underlines and affirms 'things as they are'. Popular culture is not radical; it does not seek to question or change the status quo; and it is evidence of cultural decline. On the other hand, popular culture serves to endanger social cohesion, undermine the authority of the dominant group, and generally represents a threat to traditional ways of life. If only for these reasons, then, popular culture is surely worth further study. By situating these debates in relation to more detailed discussion of economics, politics, social history and cultural theory, so media and cultural studies degrees are in a position to confront the arguments about 'Culture' and popular culture.

FURTHER READING

Storey, J. (2001), *Cultural Theory and Popular Culture: An Introduction*, 3rd edn, Harlow: Pearson Education; *http:// cwx.prenhall.com/ bookbind/pubbooks/storey_ema/ (this also has exercises, self-assessments, and glossary of key terms).

Strinati, D. (2000), *An Introduction to Studying Popular Culture*, London and New York: Routledge.

Williams, R. (1965), *The Long Revolution*, Harmondsworth: Penguin.

Williams, R. (1988; 1976), *Keywords: A Vocabulary of Culture and Society*, London: Fontana.

8 PRODUCTION AND CONSUMPTION OF MEDIA AND CULTURE

MAKING MEANINGS IN MEDIA AND CULTURAL STUDIES

Production and consumption are key terms in media and cultural studies. However, the terms do not simply refer to the products and services which the media and culture industries create for audiences or users. More complexly, production and consumption are concerned with one of the more contentious and indeed interesting areas in media and cultural studies: 'meaning'. How, then, is meaning discussed and theorised in media and cultural studies? Why is meaning an important area of discussion and debate on degree programmes in the field? Are the meanings of media and culture not self-evident because fixed? How is meaning connected to production and consumption?

The meaning of media and culture is important for a number of reasons, but three areas are worth singling out in any outline of media and cultural studies degree programmes.

1. The media are the concern of those areas of social life which deal in part with the production of representations and images. Films, television news, popular romance novels, comic books, newspapers and photographs are some of the obvious examples of how images and narratives are communicated to audiences. These images are produced, and subsequently consumed, and so the study of the processes of production and consumption are always important in deepening knowledge about the processes and functions of mass communications in society.

2. At some point, however, media representations make sense in relation to much broader discourses and ideologies in the

wider society (for example, discourses of race, of gender and of social class). In making sense of media images, and in trying to work with and understand the meanings of media representations, media analysis will need to focus directly on the discourses which surround and structure the production and consumption of media forms themselves. Thus, discourses of race and ethnicity, social class and gender and sexuality are just some of the areas which a degree in media and cultural studies will explore.

3. After taking into account the operations of discourse in the structuring of production and consumption, then analysis will need to consider the construction of meaning. Should critical analysis focus on media output (for example, the film) or should media analysis focus on what audiences do with the product (for example, audience interpretations)? If the meaning of an object is largely connected to the intentions and activities of production, then meaning will reside in the production activities and intentions themselves. But because producers make an object (for example, a television programme), so meaning must partly lie in the finished product itself. If meaning resides in the media product itself, then this will have implications on how media analysts do their research. If the making of meaning is thought to be an activity of the audience (that audiences make meanings in specific acts of cultural consumption), then clearly research will focus less on the properties of the media text and more on what audiences do with the text.

Throughout this book, much stress is placed on the importance of social, economic and historical situations in the understanding and analysis of media and culture. Whilst the media and culture have been discussed in terms of texts and output, and in terms of the activities and practices of 'everyday life', the interpretation of culture also has as its backdrop the economic and political forces in which interpretive acts occur. Moreover, the activities of consumption which are thought to mark everyday life (for example, shopping, reading or going to the cinema) are activities which are far from neutral. These activities are always motivated, taking place in relation to the discourses and ideologies which position subjects as consumers, and the economic factors which ensure that some subjects find themselves unable to consume for financial reasons. The following sections, then, provide an outline of some of the key issues and concerns which degree courses in media and cultural studies will address in relation to the study of the spheres of production and consumption.

Two-way operations

How will media and cultural studies degrees elaborate on the operations of media producers and consumers? The activities associated with production (making, constructing, inventing, creating) seem obviously opposed to those of consumption (using, expending, digesting, consuming). At the beginning of the undergraduate study of media and culture, both terms prove useful in understanding how individuals and societies produce goods and services which are subsequently consumed at the level of *use value* (the car is a means of transport) and *exchange value* (the car is a status symbol). In the case of media output, television programmes are made by production teams, and the viewers of the TV programme watch the final product. Similarly, musicians, filmmakers, record producers, radio production teams, writers, journalists and photographers produce output and texts which are subsequently listened to, watched or read.

But a fairly simple enlargement of this binary model begins to demonstrate degrees of complexity. For instance, the groups who are responsible for the production of the output (a television drama, for instance) are also themselves engaged in activities of consumption simply by using and expending the human and material resources which they do in order to produce the finished programme. Actors need to be hired; props will need to be bought; and camera equipment has to be renewed. Similarly, the audiences who are watching the drama on television are understood to watch or consume the programme, but, in the very acts of consumption, audiences are in effect producing their own readings and interpretations of what seems a finished product.

The above model of production and consumption, then, will be developed in more complex directions on degree programmes. For example, production and consumption are terms which can also be used to imagine how capitalist modes of production operate separately from modes of consumption. In many senses, the production of media and culture is or seems to be separate from its consumption. However, most consumers are also producers as well. Groups of people might be involved in the production of a particular good or service which they also consume. People who work for local authorities in a town or city are also the consumers of the service if they live in the same town. Similarly, the production of pollution (via the burning of fossil fuels, for instance) occurs in relation to the use of cars, central heating and other forms of consumption. In that sense, the terms 'production' and 'consumption', which take some of their meaning from Marxist analysis, are terms which can seem to hide the economic as well as the ideological conditions in which people are constructed as producers and not consumers, and vice versa.

Consumption-based models and the making of meaning

But production and consumption also concern other critical questions and debates in media and cultural studies. In some traditions of media and cultural theory, the emphasis on the audience's interpretation of the product or text is paramount. All texts circulate in the culture, and, whilst the writer's or author's or producer's intentions might be clear or important, there is no reason why these intentions should impact on the audience at the moment of consumption. The stress on consumption or interpretation is also a way of suggesting that the acts of interpretation are what matter in media analysis. Consumption, allied as it is to the verb 'consume' and the noun 'consumer', suggests that the text or cultural product is something which audiences actively use in the way that consumer goods are used. Consumption is understood to be an active process, something which readers or viewers choose to do. Consumption is thus a reflection of human agency and selection. A consumption-based model of cultural analysis will see audiences as active agents in the construction of the meaning of the text. In the recent past, critical perspectives, particularly in literary studies but also in some traditions in cultural studies, placed emphasis on the role of the author in the construction of meaning. An 'authorial' model will view the text's aims and intentions as solely those of the author. Thus, a play by Shakespeare or a novel by Jane Austen are thought to have the authorial imprint of the writer. Not only is the writer's style unique and identifiable, but so also is her or his intention.

There is little doubt that the writer of any text has an intention or intentions. These and similar literary works are written with a particular aim or objective in mind (for example, to entertain, to instruct), and critical analysis will want to understand the author's and the text's intentions. This can be an important task, especially in the editing of canonical literature and the compilation of definitive editions (for example, the works of James Joyce and George Eliot have proved interesting in this regard) or in the staging of plays (for example, Samuel Beckett and Bertolt Brecht leave fairly precise notes about how the works will be performed). However, a number of problems emerge if the text is understood simply in terms of its authorial or uniquely textual intentions. Films and television dramas, for example, involve many people, and so a single intention or meaning is never straightforward. Moreover, historical contexts complicate matters further.

If texts are to be understood in relation to the historical contexts of their production, then material 'outside' the text, particularly specific historical circumstances or events, will clearly have some bearing on the production of what goes on 'in' the text or on how it is decoded. On the one hand, it will be important to consider whether the text reflects the history in which it is produced, and on the other hand it might also be important to consider the degree to which the text challenges this history. We can consider, for instance, the work of Mary Shelley. Her novel *Frankenstein* might not seem a particularly feminist novel. We know, for instance, that it emerged from spoken accounts which were told in the presence of others, and that the story was subsequently made into the novel we read today. But an examination of the novel's own historicity would suggest that it is not simply a story about a doctor who creates a monster. Rather, it is equally concerned with the rights of women in the early nineteenth century, as well as the spread and force of capitalism and industrialisation. How far do readers of the novel need to know this kind of information? Does lack of this kind of knowledge generate a limited interpretation? Following a consumption-based model of cultural analysis, then texts are made to mean what they do mean in the circumstances not just of the writer but also of the reader. Thus, meaning is always a dual process of production and consumption, not something wholly controlled by the producer.

Other factors, however, impact on how texts are read and interpreted. For example, all texts have *implied* and *actual* readers or audiences. The implied reader is the one who emerges from the text itself, the one who, in effect, is created by the text. It is the implied reader whose support is enlisted in the unfolding of the story, a reader who is imagined via the text's way of addressing its audience. The actual reader is the one who, in reading, also brings to bear her or his own wealth of experience. So meaning is not simply something which is imposed but is rather, on the consumption-centred model, that which emerges on the basis of an oscillation which implicates readers, texts and contexts. In the activity of reading, readers concretise the text in relation to their own experience of reality as well as the experiences of other readers.

If textual meaning is fixed, either in relation to the text itself or in relation to the author, then meaning, although embedded in text and/or author, is able to transcend the bounds of history and require no interpretation. In some traditions of critical and literary inquiry, certain texts are thought to possess such transcendental or eternal qualities. This is of course an extreme version of the author model, but one which nonetheless is worth bearing in mind in any arguments on undergraduate programmes which deal with tradition, cultural heritage and history.

Production-based models and the making of meaning

Degree courses in cultural studies will address issues of production and consumption in relation to a range of topics. Production degrees are those which deal mainly with training students in the critical and practical skills of working in the media production industries. So production in a very basic sense means working in fields such as video and radio production, sound and recording, journalism, digital media and web-based media. You will find that media production modules require students to work in teams, so that more than one person is always involved in the production of meaning. However, advertising, shopping, fashion, youth cultures and subcultures, and popular music are some of the topics and concepts which concern production and consumption. Modules in these areas will make direct reference to specific theories and encourage students to discuss and debate the politics of culture in relation to the forces of production and consumption.

At first sight, this might seem a strange way to consider production and consumption. For example, films, television programmes, CDs, videos, DVDs and games do not have one sole author or producer. A film has a producer but it often has hundreds of other people who will contribute to the making of the piece. *Doctor Who* is a popular sci-fi series which has run intermittently on BBC television since the early 1960s. A number of writers have been involved in the series, an even larger number of people have worked on the production of the series, and an equally large number of characters have acted in the popular drama. To imagine, however, that there is a final meaning to any single episode is to limit how the programme is understood or used in the culture. On one level, the series is understood within the genres of sci-fi as well as 'children's' television. These genre boundaries, therefore, serve to limit the range of meanings any programme will have. And to the extent that genre is determined in relation to the making of the programme, then clearly the production side of meaning is important. Genres not only package the meanings of the text (for example, sci-fi, romance or horror), but also make assumptions about how human experience is or is not subject to packaging.

One way of understanding the role of the production-side in the twofold determination of meanings is to consider film, cinema and the Hollywood system which typified production practices during the early part of the twentieth century. During this period, the corporations (for example, MGM, Paramount, Warner Bros.), closely allied with the studio system, integrated fully all aspects of production, distribution and exhibition. 'Universal' and 'Columbia' focused on production and distribution, and United Artists saw mainly to distribution. This system operated to keep competitors out of the film and cinema industry. Moreover, the studio system itself meant high degrees of both specialisation and the division of labour. Film production was thus shared across teams of highly specialist workers. Although the finished product, the film, is always open to various meanings and interpretations, the realities of production meant that cultural production occurred for reasons of ongoing reproduction and profit. Specialisation and the division of labour, therefore, frequently ensured that workers' own creativity and potential was always harnessed to the demands of a system whose logic was profit and the ever-increasing efficiency of the system. These production frameworks, and the refinement of popular genres, also meant that films were produced in very familiar ways. Predictable camera movement and editing, and equally predictable plots, sequences, scripts and endings ensured that the meanings of films seemed wholly determined in relation to the term 'Hollywood', a description which was increasingly used to define a highly structured system of cultural production.

Of course, media and cultural studies degree programmes will complicate the above details, showing how the drive for profit does not necessarily frustrate those in culture who would seek to subvert its powerful force. Moreover, the obligation to make profit is not something without its own contradictions. Indeed, throughout the history of culture and popular culture, it can be seen that the latter version, especially during the eighteenth and nineteenth centuries, is something which emerges in opposition to a culture whose economic conditions could not ultimately control cultural and social antagonism. Thus, studies of production and consumption on cultural and media degree programmes will cover historical as well as contemporary examples in the analysis of how meanings are made and remade in social life.

FURTHER READING

Storey, J. (1999), *Cultural Consumption and Everyday Life*, London: Arnold.
Strinati, D. (2000), *An Introduction to Studying Popular Culture*, London and New York: Routledge.

9 SUBCULTURES

DOMINANCE AND RESISTANCE IN CULTURE

If culture means 'way of life', is there a dominant way of life in all societies? If 'yes', then are there subordinate or *subcultures* in all societies? How might groups challenge the dominant culture, and why might it be challenged? How is political protest or resistance expressed in culture? Is culture, a way of life, something which is fixed by a dominant group and which other groups have to endorse? Or is culture always in processes of change? Are some cultures more privileged than others? Do some groups seem to have more power over culture than others? How are subcultures identified? Do clothes, facial makeup, tattoos or hairstyles matter in the culture? How do cultures change? These questions are not new, but they remain important on cultural and media studies degrees to the extent that culture is 'political', with a lower-case as well as a capital 'P'.

Variations on these questions – in relation to political and social change – were being asked long before media and cultural studies began to examine what are now known as subcultures. Political and social thinkers, activists on the left, philosophers and historians have always been interested in change and conflict in society. Some critical and theoretical traditions are interested simply in the very processes of change. Other groups and traditions are committed to revolutionary social change. These different traditions and constituencies offer competing solutions as to how change might come about. During the nineteenth century, philosopher and social theorist Karl Marx based an entire economic and political philosophy on the absolute necessity of changing capitalist modes of production. Indeed, Marxist theory and criticism remains an important and powerful critical tradition in cultural analysis, and it is one which continues to underpin very powerful and convincing analyses of culture, society and the media.

During the early part of the twentieth century, Italian Marxist-activist Antonio Gramsci sought to explain how Marx's theory of revolution might be understood not just in economic and structural terms, but in terms of what can be referred to as 'Cultural Politics'. A Gramscian approach to cultural studies can be formulated in terms of questions such as the following. How is conflict measured in culture? Does cultural conflict imply a need to change the culture? Who brings about such change? Who stands in a position of leadership in culture, and are these leaders the ones who inaugurate change? In a way, his questions and his discussions represent an attempt to understand how culture – a way of life – is composed of elements which reflect the conflicts and divisions of the economy. Simply stated, a way of life is constituted in terms of a dominant (and thus a potentially 'leading' group) and a subordinate (and thus a potentially dominated) group. On a media and cultural studies degree, his arguments and the refinements to them, will be subject to important scrutiny, complication and debate. But Gramsci is mentioned at the outset of this short section on subcultures because of his formulation of the notion of 'hegemony' or leadership in culture. Gramsci's questions are important, and they are not solely related to subcultures. However, one way of understanding something of hegemony is in the field of subcultural studies.

Culture, tradition, history

The preceding questions, and their many answers, will be considered in any undergraduate module dealing with a branch of media and cultural studies referred to as 'subcultures'. The study of subcultures is not the same as, but often includes, the investigation of youth cultures, club cultures, fashion, style, popular fiction and reading, and popular music. In some theoretical perspectives, the analysis of media and culture is, either by default or by intention, the analysis of subcultures. During the 1970s, Birmingham University's Centre for Contemporary Cultural Studies (CCCS) undertook a range of research projects which investigated the relations between social class, everyday rituals and subcultures. From this research, subcultures can be defined as groups of people whose views and values are in conflict with, deviate from or actively distort the dominant practices of the leading group in the culture.

One way of understanding subcultures is via the CCCS's own emphasis on the importance of ethnographic research into subcultures. The research of the CCCS did not discover a harmonious, cohesive British culture, but one which was composed of various groups engaged in cultural 'struggle' and 'resistance' (the terms are always relative to the context). Subcultures during the period circa 1955 to 1980 are thought to reflect various forms of resistance and subversion, evidenced in cultural practices which link dress, fashion and particular styles to identity formations and subcultural communities. These subcultural identities (skinhead and punk subcultures are among the most frequently cited) are thus reflections of cultural and social contradictions in the dominant culture. In subcultural studies, symbolic resistance and refusal are as much expressive of the subculture as they are an articulation of much wider cultural and political conflicts. But subculture study raises more questions about the study of the media and culture.

Who asks the questions?

The terms 'culture', 'Culture', 'cultures' and 'cultural' have been used throughout this book in order to provide a sense of how, in describing and analysing social experience, certain words serve to frame how we understand the world of that experience. Popular culture does not describe a separate domain to the one signified in the term 'high culture' so much as it can often serve to create the very distinction it seems to describe. Words such as the 'economy' or 'society' are deployed not to depict a different world, one which is somehow not cultural, so much as they are the technical words which are mobilised in order to perceive and to visualise the world in different terms.

Moreover, it has been stressed that 'culture' can signify in singular and plural ways. In its singular usage, culture can mean a whole way of life. But once a specific way of life is analysed or discussed, then it fast becomes a concern about plural, multiple and competing cultures. Cultural difference, then, is not simply that which emerges when two apparently different cultures are contrasted one with the other. Medieval European cultures inevitably do seem different to the cultures which are articulated and expressed today. Moreover, accounts of twentieth-century Western European cultures are not the same as, and are motivated by a research logic which might be distinctly different to, those documented by anthropologists working in (so-called) 'developing' countries. So cultural difference, then, can be understood in terms of historical as well as cultural-geographical and spatial contrast. In the case of historical comparison, then, it may well be that European cultures of the present are seen to be continuous with those of the past.

In the case of cross-cultural comparisons, then, difference has traditionally been understood and measured on the basis of ethnographic and anthropological inquiry. A key area which degree programmes might develop will relate to research methodology. The method which is used in the analysis of culture will always attend to questions of ownership and control. Who, for instance, is in a position to ask questions about culture in the first instance, and how are they in the position to frame and ask the questions they do? Why are the questions being asked, and how are the findings being used? Being in a position to do research or to ask questions in this way implies a position of dominance. Some traditions of research were grounded in colonialist models of social inquiry. This meant that the researchers who went into the culture often assumed the host culture was the alien one, whereas the culture of the researchers was somehow superior.

However, whenever cultures and subcultures are subjected to detailed analysis, it becomes difficult to posit a *dominant* culture in any simple sense and, by extension, to posit a subculture or subordinate culture. The 'culture' is not something which is fixed to or contained in an object or a group so much as it is associated with discourses which combine to construct culture at any one moment. One of the most intriguing aspects of cultural studies is that it is the study of an entity (way of life) which, in practice, is also the study of the processes of living according to sets of conventions (how to dress, where to shop, how to speak, what to read, who to socialise with and so on). But because the historical analysis of culture seems to suggest that these conventions are not easily agreed, then the study of a way of life is also the study of the politics and the conflicts of culture. Hence, the questions asked on degree programmes are deeply relevant to the understanding of social relationships and the kinds of political constraints which structure these relationships on an everyday basis.

Inbuilt conflicts

Cross-cultural and subcultural research raises important questions. For instance, why is cultural difference being measured, and how is the data being used? Are questions raised about cultural sameness? How are questions about cultural difference or sameness framed, and from whose perspective are two cultures measured? What is the motivation which propels cross-cultural research in the first instance? Media and cultural studies courses emerge out of predominantly Western discourses and Western universities. In that sense, media and cultural studies will inevitably use a language which makes sense to its own audiences in the West. This form of inbuilt 'bias' or positionality is in certain respects unavoidable, but it is one which nonetheless will always underpin how research questions are framed at the start of any project. But media and cultural studies, from the beginnings of their formations as academic disciplines, have undertaken research which has been underpinned by the premise that what seems to unite cultures is as interesting as what seems to separate cultures. These unities and separations are, in a sense, evident in the interdisciplinary nature of media and cultural studies degrees as well as cultural and media research.

What these preceding observations hopefully indicate is that Culture with a capital 'C' is not something which exists outside its own historical formation. Culture, still with a capital letter, is an object of inquiry that is both constructed (determined by methods) and yet seemingly essential (it is possible to identify the cultural history of all societies). But cultural history seems to suggest that all ways of life are marked by conflict and division. Subcultures, then, are those formations which rely on the dominant culture at the same time as they contest its hegemony and power, often in acts which express conflict.

In many ways it is through Raymond Williams's work that the study of Antonio Gramsci was introduced into British cultural studies. In Williams's reading of this history of Western culture, the dominant culture consists of the central as well as the dominant systems of making meaning. The dominant culture, though constructed, is not an abstract idea but is expressed in relation to the culture's values. But Williams, carefully following Gramsci's lead, shows how all dominant cultures are composed of competing forces. The dominant culture is always threatened by alternative, emergent or oppositional cultures. The dominant culture may tolerate opposition, but it may equally suppress, stifle or incorporate the competing cultural formations. But for the dominant culture to sustain itself, it has to exercise a hegemony or leadership which is without any apparent fractures or breaks. In other words, the dominant culture has always to justify itself by redefining and defending itself. But this is both a strenuous and an almost impossible task.

Some meanings of style

One way of understanding the dynamics of dominant, residual, resistant and emergent cultures is via the study of subcultures. One of the first and most interesting accounts of youth subcultures is Phil Cohen's study of a working-class district in the East End of London. Using metaphors to describe the activities of parent and youth cultures, Cohen's is an account which explores the relationship between class and social change. During the 1950s, working-class communities had to face two challenges. First, Britain's political leaders promoted the UK as an affluent, progressive, capitalist economy. The new affluence was represented in terms of consumption and spending power. Secondly, structural changes in the economy, alongside the move to new housing developments destabilised working-class life. One way in which young people responded to these competing ideologies of progress and affluence on the one hand, and the traditions of working-class family life on the other, was via the subculture. Cohen cites as his examples the 'mods', 'parkas', 'skinheads' and 'crombies', all of whom took from the parent culture those elements which sustained, for the subculture, a sense of community and tradition. But these same subcultures appropriated elements of the affluent society, signalling a symbolic engagement with the emerging discourse of the consumer.

A later study, Dick Hebdige's *Subculture: The Meaning of Style* (1979) draws on a range of work in semiotics, sociology and literary studies to provide another theorisation of subcultures. Hebdige suggests that a key activity of subcultures is the group's use and appropriation of commodities, and its reworking of contemporary fashions and styles which marks the subculture off from the parent or dominant culture. He shows how, in the subculture's acts of 'bricolage', individual objects (for example, items of clothing or other products) are removed from their original contexts and appropriated by the subculture for other purposes and in different – subcultural – contexts.

More recent work on fan cultures makes links with subcultural analysis, showing how fandom can operate in oppositional ways. If societies, particularly in the West, construct audiences on the basis of mass spectatorship (for example, the televisual event), then fan cultures serve to contest this (apparent) passivity of the spectator by using texts, not to venerate them but in the ongoing reformation of culture. But fandom's appropriation of the media in this way also suggests that it is the mass media which help to shape the fan subculture. Subcultures, while they might make claims about identity and authenticity, are derived from the mixing and blending of consumer products. The claims to authenticity are, nonetheless, important. Although the subculture is no more or less authentic than the dominant culture, the claim to authenticity is a way of registering the group's attachment to particular identities and identifications. These alliances allow subjects to negotiate and affirm varying degrees of cultural and social difference.

The study of fandom is something most media and cultural studies degrees will encourage, and level III students are able to develop an interest in detailed ways via the dissertation. Similarly, dissertations which carry out research into subcultures often demonstrate really interesting links between cultural politics, theory and the subculture itself. Alternatively, media production students might want to consider making a radio or television programme which examines the visual and musical aspects of youth subcultures in the university town. Level III projects often expose some of the internal differences which mark subcultures, exploring the details of a subculture's specific history and identity. Undergraduate studies might also want to ask whether subcultures feature in contemporary cultures in the way that they did in the recent past. Questions about what is mainstream, marginal, dominant or subordinate in the culture are far from straightforward, and it might well be that cultural formations are better understood using other analytic frameworks. Finally, it may be the case that all subjects, for different reasons, are marginal and mainstream in different ways at any one time. In which case, then media and cultural studies degrees still have much to contribute to the ongoing debates surrounding subcultures.

FURTHER READING

Hebidge, D. (1979), *Subculture: The Meaning of Style*, London: Methuen.
Willis, P. (1990), *Common Culture*, Milton Keynes: Open University Press.

10   MEDIA: METHODS OF ANALYSIS

WHY MEDIA ANALYSIS?

We have seen throughout Part II of this book that media analysis is interested in understanding advertising and consumption, audiences, communication technologies, broadcasting, globalisation, institutions and values, and ideologies and representations. How, then, are these areas analysed? What strategies might be adopted in understanding and measuring the mass media? In any discipline studied at university, there are a number of competing theories which can be used in the analysis of the field, and a short introduction such as this will only outline some of the general trends and directions in media analysis. However, the rationale which underpins the Get Set series of book is one which seeks to prepare students for the specific demands of the degree programme and, in the process, to highlight good practice in study and research skills in media and culture. This particular chapter, then, seeks to underline the importance of media analysis at the same time as encouraging students to use general and specific sources of data in the production of essays.

Later in this chapter, references are made to a recent journal article dealing with media analysis. Journal articles can be accessed in libraries as well as electronically. Of course, the media and cultural studies shelves in libraries house many sources, including books, newspapers, journals, abstracts and indexes. Computers are also vital to media analysis, providing access to databases, electronic journals and other useful sources. It is important that these sources are used to the full. However, this part of the book aims to show how journal articles are potentially very accessible and useful sources of information. Journals might appear intimidating if you have never used them before, but they can be vital in work produced at levels II and III as well as in a dissertation. The specialist nature of the journal or the journal article means that you can structure your work in relation to the details of recent research rather than simply on the basis of textbook summaries, important though the latter sources are. Accessing journal articles, moreover, is becoming much easier in university libraries. Many journals are available electronically as 'e-journals'. Each university library will have different systems in place, though data access is fairly straightforward (via computers), and can be managed using keyword searches or searching the A–Z catalogue of e-journals (also available on the library computers). In addition, databases in the arts, humanities and social sciences prove invaluable in undertaking similar searches. Be encouraged, therefore, to pursue these activities as soon as you are introduced to library information systems.

The importance of media analysis, alongside a brief summary of qualitative and quantitative research methods, was outlined in Chapter 1, 'What Are the Media? What Is Media Studies?' But why is media analysis undertaken, and what sorts of questions are asked? Throughout much of the twentieth century, media analysis was concerned with the effects of the media on behaviour, and, with the arrival of television, research often focused on representations of violence. But will the analysis of violence on television tell us about programmes, about audiences or about the complex interoperation of media output on the audience? Media analysis examines issues which include the effects of the media on behaviour, on decision making and on voting intentions. But what does media analysis tell us about the impact of the media on human relationships and how these relationships are perceived? Is the media so all powerful and all pervasive that it is indifferent to critical and theoretical analysis, and potentially indifferent to reform or change?

These last questions surely indicate that media literacy and media analysis are vital to the understanding of human relationships in contemporary societies. This is why media analysis will form a key part of all degree programmes. Modules with titles such as 'Politics, Representation and the Mass Media', 'Alternative Media', 'Media Ethics' or 'Globalisation and the Media' will probably address the pressing issues which surround the media today. More general media studies courses will introduce topics such as content analysis, frame analysis, effects models, active audience research and ethnography. But media content analysis, for instance, can also be undertaken in relation to audience studies as much as it can be undertaken in relation to semiotics. Feminist research, sexuality studies and postcolonial studies will also play a part in shaping how media is both selected for analysis and how it is analysed.

Contexts for/of media analysis

Before looking in detail at the journal article concerned with media research methods, we can usefully gain some insight into the breadth and dimensions of research by looking at a more general study. Often, quantitative media research is undertaken for specific organisations and groups, or is commissioned by governments, funding councils and research bodies. For example, the American Psychological Association in 1986 appointed a research committee to investigate and review the relationship between television and society, particularly the 'psychosocial effects' of television. The study's findings were published with the University of Nebraska under the title *Big World, Small Screen: The Role of Television in American Society* (Huston, 1992). This research is referred to here in order that students of media studies are able to gain a sense of some of the key issues involved in quantitative media research. It is also a research project which draws on a range of other disciplines and theories (for example, psychology, discourse studies) in order to undertake the research and present its findings.

Alongside the exploration of television's deployment of stereotypes, and the 'impact of television' on specific social groups, members of the research panel were required to review and assess how television influences social and personal relationships, intellectual and cognitive functioning, emotional development, and feelings and attitudes towards family, gender and sexuality. Regardless of how the research findings are phrased or ultimately assessed, vital though such questions are, the study is useful for students because it provides a sense of the principal themes and social and theoretical contexts of quantitative and qualitative media analysis.

'Impure' media theory

Students of media studies will also be interested in how this and similar research underlines media analysis's indebtedness to the fields of sociology, psychology, linguistics and psycholinguistics, and anthropology. Students taking a media studies degree will often move outside the specific field of media studies and confront ideas from other subject disciplines. But what the study also reveals is how these fields have informed and shaped media theory's own specific frames of reference and analysis. Whilst, then, the findings of the research panel are certainly open to further question, and students would be encouraged to discuss and appraise the research itself critically, the methods to which the research refers typify how media analysis can be undertaken.

Throughout the study, fairly direct reference is made to research methods and media analyses, and these may be listed as: agenda setting, audience measurement, effects research, content analysis, cultivation analysis, demographic analysis, uses and gratifications, ethnography, participant observation, media literacy analysis, mass observation and large-scale correlation studies. Reference is made to television and consumption behaviour, discourse analysis, evaluative assertion analysis, frame analysis, genre theory and narratology. Alongside the approaches mentioned above however, it is to be underlined that many in media studies would adopt other approaches to media analysis, and so students should be prepared to confront a range of traditions and perspectives in the first year of study.

The list of research methods above is fairly extensive and it represents a tradition of media analysis which is interested in defining with some *objectivity* (the term and the aim is always problematic) what is thought to happen (in terms of behaviour, perceptions and intentions) when 'people' watch television. The study makes reference to the specific economic and social conditions of the audience as well as to other aspects of identity (for example, gender, ethnicity). This kind of approach to media analysis is broadly linked to effects research, a tradition which perceives the media in terms of its impact and influence over audiences. Effects research is also underpinned by specific traditions in psychology and sociology in which the individual and the audience are viewed in terms of their susceptibility or responsiveness to representations of violence and aggression. The effects tradition is quite different to some of the analytic trajectories in media studies which draw on cultural studies or interpretive methods. These last approaches to the media (see the work of Ien Ang, Joke Hermes and David Morley) tend to stress an individual's or group's agency or power in a model of the media which emphasises the audience's negotiation and interpretation of output, particularly in the spheres of representation and media consumption.

Media analysis, whichever method is used, is never objective in any straightforward or non-subjective sense. Your degree course will surely make arguments for and against 'objectivity', and so it is important to confront the issue early in the course. Moreover, courses will also argue that perhaps the old divisions between quantitative and qualitative methodologies are no longer tenable. These are important debates, and will be discussed in detail at level II or III. However, analytic methods associated with content analysis, texts, ethnography, uses and gratifications, or agenda setting can produce different findings using the same data. Equally, ethnography and audience studies, whilst they might seem to be eliciting the views of audiences on the basis of some investigative disinterestedness, must first of all establish a research agenda where specific interview questions are formulated, overarching theories endorsed and specific audiences sought. In addition, for every method of media analysis, assumptions are made about audiences or the group being identified for research purposes. Media analysis, far from discovering a truth, is itself engaged in the construction or framing of truths on the basis of the analytic methods and theoretical perspectives it adopts. The reporting and portrayal of the news 'as it happens' is impossible. The Glasgow Media Group have spent much time analysing how editing, selection, perspective, technology and government regulations all position the news long before it is transmitted. A chapter such as this, however, can only briefly assess some of the methods that have proved useful for past and ongoing media research. Needless to say, broad coverage is provided, and students are encouraged to extend and develop initial analyses and interests on the basis of further reading, research and critical application.

CONTENT AND FRAME ANALYSIS

This part of the chapter summarises how a journal article has discussed 'content analysis'. The article on content analysis is interesting because it shows how computers, ICT and databases are both very useful and increasingly essential in media analysis. The second part of this section introduces some of the key ways of using frame analysis.

Content analysis

Content analysis in media studies is deployed in order to determine 'how much of what sort of content is sent and how much of what sort is received by whom' (McQuail, 1992: 177). Content analysis is thought to inform media researchers and analysts of how much of a particular representation (for example, violence, stereotyping, pornography) is in a sample of programmes. On a more complex level, content analysis has to be understood in relation to the responses, readings and interpretations of media audiences. In the case of the Glasgow University Media Group, content is analysed in order to expose surface or obvious content as well as in-depth or hidden content. Output is subsequently examined and its impact assessed in relation to variables such as audiences, industrial relations, policy and media power. The stress in quantitative content analysis is broadly positivistic, an approach which measures or counts the quantity of media communication in relation to types or series of responses. The underlying premise of content analysis is that an exploration and analysis of media communications and messages can provide information about the audiences who receive and use the messages.

While quantitative content analysis will always be used in conjunction with other analytic approaches, the procedure for content analysis is usefully summarised by McQuail:

(1) choose a universe or sample of content; (2) establish a category frame of external referents relevant to the purpose of the inquiry . . . (3) choose a 'unit of analysis' from the content . . . (4) match content to category frame, per chosen unit of content; (5) express the result as an overall distribution of the total universe of sample in terms of the frequency of occurrence of the sought-for-referents. (183)

The approach outlined by McQuail is the method adopted in many analyses, though different research aims will define how the content analysis is undertaken. The broadly empiricist approach summarised by McQuail has been supplemented in a number of ways, particularly by cultural analyses of media output. However, since the 1970s, Glasgow University Media Group has undertaken quantitative with qualitative analyses of the reporting of British and international conflict. Their findings underline the mass media's continuing power in the mobilisation of public opinion.

But content analysis continues to be used in wide-ranging ways. A research project, undertaken by David Bengston and David Fan, examined conflict over natural resource management using 'computer-coded content analysis of news media stories to measure the relative level of conflict related to policy and management of the U.S. national forests from 1992 through 1996' (Bengston and Fan, 1998: 494). The article by Bengston and Fan has been chosen in order to encourage students to access journal articles and electronic resources. Content analysis in their study was developed in order to identify evidence of conflict in a database of news media text. The researchers' analyses of changes in the quantity of media discussion surrounding conflict were logged over a specific period of time so that comparisons could be made.

Their procedure for data collection entailed the following six stages and it usefully illustrates strategies for content analysis:

1. news media stories concerning natural resource management were collected over a five-year period;

2. news media stories were downloaded from key commercial databases;

3. key reference sources were used in the identification of all news sources;

4. the researchers identified thirty-three news sources which included US national newspapers, news wires and television and radio news transcripts;

5. the news sources were searched using keywords and commands such as '[(Forest Service) or (national forest)]'; and

6. the searches were encoded so as to eliminate irrelevant stories so that only text within the parameters of the phrases was downloaded.

The aims of this research, and of content analysis in general, are not simply to amass data. Rather, Bengston and Fan identified first of all three key objectives surrounding the content analysis. First, they seek to assess the success or otherwise of new policies which are supposed to conflict. In addition, their work monitors the levels of conflict associated with specific issues. And, finally, they warn policymakers about issues newly emerging in relation to forest conflict. In order to achieve these aims, the collection and subsequent analysis of content was undertaken in relation to a list of key terms, words and phrases. This meant the researchers had to produce a series of computer rules which were used in order to identify words and expressions specifically concerned with forest conflict. The development of this dictionary involved an 'iterative' process. The initial dictionary of terms, phrases and coding rules was later refined in order to exclude as far as possible any ambiguity in the collection and analysis of key data. Phrases and expressions that were discovered to be used in ambiguous or incorrect ways for the purposes of the research were abandoned. The final dictionary contained seven key conflict terms. However, the dictionary and its application in the analysis of conflict was continuously refined so that a greater-than 80 per cent degree of accuracy was achieved.

The research of Bengston and Fan shows how content analysis of media discourse can be broken down into individual issues, thus making it possible to monitor the level of conflict in a specific field. Simply recording the amount of times search terms generate positive results makes no sense outside the analytic frame in which the content is collected. In measuring data of the kind they did, the researchers were clear that they were also working with news media in relation to agenda setting, policy evaluation, social conflict and the management of space and natural resources in a major global economy. Here, we can see the importance of media analysis, not just to the understanding of the impact of news media, but in terms of the impact of the news in relation to globalisation.

Frame analysis

Bengston and Fan's research is concerned with the analysis of news media. Similarly, the Glasgow Media Group is associated with the analysis of news, current affairs and documentary programmes. Programmes within this genre have also been analysed in relation to frame analysis, a method (also used in visual as well as conversation analysis) which sets out to understand media representations in relation to the structuring, sequencing and narrativisation of the news. The starting question for frame analysis is, at the initial stage of analysis, fairly obvious: how is media output made to represent and construct reality? The terms which phrase this question also indicate its potential complexity. 'Represent', 'construct' and 'reality' are always contentious and far from obvious. While frame analysis, therefore, deals with the narrative construction of the 'news', what makes the news is always subject to institutional and ideological regulation.

Frame analysis, frequently used for television and visual analysis, can be understood in relation to the beginning and end of a news broadcast, the sequencing of items within the news broadcast, and overall thematic stresses within the broadcast. Consider the following analytic progression:

1. How long is the news broadcast (for example, fifteen minutes, thirty minutes)?

2. How is the news opened, developed and closed (for example, images, pictures, titles, sound, etc.)?

3. How do the newsreaders, the opening pictures, the images and all the material used prior to the opening of the first report establish and sequence the news agenda for that broadcast?

4. Are individual reports (for example, first news report, second news report, etc.) established inside studio, presented as 'live', arranged around or with reporters, interviews, etc.?

5. Consider the use of represented groups, individuals, personal narratives, dramatic effects, tone of voice, etc., in the construction and framing of news.

6. What other material is used in the report that might link with other themes or issues in the news?

Using this introductory model, we can see that to 'frame' something for analysis is, as the term suggests, to choose some aspect of reality and isolate it in a particular way or casing. Frame analysis, then, provides a sense of how a particular reality is put together in relation to a fourfold equation which:

1. provides an the outline of problem;

2. presents the findings on the basis of investigations;

3. conducts further analyses, observations and scrutiny of initial findings;

4. makes a judgement on the findings of the frame analysis and suggests provisional conclusions.

A principal objective in frame analysis is to understand the relationship between the media organisation (for example, BBC), the news and the values which link these alignments in the selection of news items and the construction of an agenda. A detailed analysis of media frames can shed light on the exact ways information and communication systems, and messages, impact on human behaviour and relationships. By comparing one TV news broadcast with another, and by subsequently comparing both these with, for example, a radio news broadcast or the treatment of the same item of news in another medium, it is possible to observe how the above equation is worked out – transferred or communicated – in news productions. This will allow the frames to be seen in relation to agenda-setting and organisations or networks. In addition, agendas can be considered and questions asked about why they are framed and set in the respective media. This kind of analysis can provide insights into the policies of the organisation as much as the ways in which the news is framed. Finally, frame analysis of the kind outlined above will begin to expose the extent to which all news and indeed all media output is subject to 'ideological framing' of some kind. All media messages 'interpellate' or address audiences on the basis of the images and voices of the personal frame, and frame analysis is one way of examining which subjects are in and out of the frame at any one point.

The importance of media analysis

All media analysis has a context and a purpose. And all media analysis attempts to measure the media, its forms and its messages in relation to the public and personal spheres of audiences. However, media analysis is also concerned with representations, and with the political and ideological dimensions of all media messages. In discussions of television images or radio news reports, for instance, media analysis will seek to investigate how representations in all media also operate to symbolise power. Media analysis is interested in how subjects and groups are represented and valued in the text or medium. Thus, media analysis is not simply about how to examine the media. It is equally about understanding the media's power in the shaping of social reality. Media analysis seeks to understand who is involved in the production and representation of social life. Analysis of news reports, television output or radio, for instance, is important because of the specific ways in which people are depicted. A degree programme in media and cultural studies, then, will acquaint students with knowledge of how to conduct analysis of texts at the same time as assisting students in understanding the ways in which media texts relate to the societies in which they are received.

FURTHER READING

Ang, I. (1985), *Watching Dallas*, London: Methuen.

Bengston, D. N. and Fan, D. P. (1999), 'Conflict over Natural Resource management: A Social Indicator on Analysis of Online News Media Text', *Society and Natural Resources*, 12: 493–500.

Berger, A. A. (1982), *Media Analysis Techniques*, London: Sage.

Chomsky, N. (1991), *Deterring Democracy*, London and New York: Verso.

Chomsky, N. and Herman, E. S. (1988), *Manufacturing Consent: The Political Economy of the Mass Media*, New York: Pantheon.

Entman, R. M. (1993), 'Framing: Towards Clarification of a Fractured Paradigm', *Journal of Communication*, 43(4): 51–8.

Garnham, N. (1979), 'Contribution to a Political Economy of Mass Communication', *Media, Culture and Society*, 1 (2): 123–46.

Glasgow Media Group (1985), *War and Peace News*, London: Routledge and Kegan Paul.

Gripsrud, J. (2000), *Understanding Media Culture*, London: Hodder Arnold.

Huston, A. C. (1992), *Big World, Small Screen: The Role of Television in American Society*, Lincoln and London: University of Nebraska Press.

Iyengar, S. (1991), *Is Anyone Responsible? How Television Frames Political Issues*, Chicago: University of Chicago Press.

McCullagh, C. (2002), *Media Power: A Sociological Introduction*, Basingstoke: Palgrave Macmillan.

McQuail, D. (1992 (1983)), *Mass Communication Theory: An Introduction*, 2nd edn, London: Sage.

Watson, J. (1998), *Media Communication: An Introduction to Theory and Process*, Basingstoke and London: Macmillan, now Palgrave Macmillan.

11 THEORIES OF CULTURAL ANALYSIS

DEVELOPING THEORIES

'Theory' means many things. However, the term to which it is often opposed – practice – does not provide a sense of how theory is constructed and operates in cultural studies. In addition, practice is not something which is outside, or beyond, theory and vice versa. Theories (for example, of culture, of art, of knowledge, of the economy) are used to explain phenomena; theory is a way of accounting for an object in different terms (for example, a Marxist theory of culture compared to a psychoanalytic account); and theory is a way of intervening in culture at the same time as it is a way of metaphorically standing outside culture (seeing it in one way and not another). With theory, for instance, a way of life – a culture – is made more intelligible than if theory was not used at all. Theory is used in cultural studies, then, to construct and understand the world rather than establish facts about the world. 'Truth' is central to all theorisation, but theory does not point in the direction of one truth or fact. Theory in cultural studies frames and structures how the world is perceived and conceptualised. Frameworks such as Marxism, structuralism, political economy, feminism, deconstruction and discourse theory ensure that 'facts' are not presented as the truth of something, but as one way of understanding the construction of truths and facts.

The range of theories which are used in cultural studies is vast, so much so that it is likely that the degree programme you study will have at least one module devoted to the study of cultural theory. Some of the theories and theorists have already been referred to in this book. The work of Roland Barthes, Stuart Hall, Raymond Williams, Antonio Gramsci, Karl

Marx, Ferdinand de Saussure and others can be described as cultural theory. However, work which is referred to as cultural theory was not necessarily written as that. Moreover, the people who are referred to as 'theorists' did not set out to write theory in the way that the label 'cultural theory' might imply. Marx was a philosopher who theorised the workings of the economy in capitalist societies. Williams, for instance, who was influenced by Marx's work, combines other theories besides those of Marx in his writings. Similarly, Stuart Hall takes from Williams, Marx and Gramsci and blends their work with the structuralist theories of de Saussure.

Thus, there is not 'one' theory in cultural theory. There are, however, key positions or trajectories, some of which have already been mentioned. For instance, the work of de Saussure is broadly associated with a structuralist analysis of culture. It was structuralist theory which influenced Barthes's work in semiotics, although it is also clear that Barthes is alert to other traditions in his writings. He draws on notions of ideology which are taken from Marxist analyses of culture, but he also works with themes which typify psychoanalytic readings of culture, especially the work of Sigmund Freud and Jacques Lacan. In addition, feminist activism and criticism has added to how theory is understood so that questions of gender in human relations are central to how culture and society are theorised. Moreover, ethnicity, sexuality and social class impact on how theory formulates its questions. However, to list here all the theories studied on degree programmes would not necessarily provide an insight into how theory functions in cultural studies. The best way to work with theory is perhaps to bring together some of the points which have been made in earlier parts of the book. This will allow us to develop some key points about the usefulness of theory in cultural studies, and to sense the impact of theory in enriching all critical work in cultural studies.

CULTURE AND SIGN SYSTEMS: BACK TO THE BEGINNING

The analysis of media and cultural practices in traditions associated with cultural studies is alert to the need for quantitative and qualitative measurements along lines suggested in the preceding chapter, 'Media: Methods of Analysis'. However, in cultural studies, theoretical work has been interested in interpreting texts and audiences, in understanding how signs impact on the meanings which are given to everyday life, and in deciphering how mundane activities such as reading and eating are bound up with issues which concern nationhood, identity and conflict. It is to be recalled that in the work of Roland Barthes, cultural analysis is not solely concerned with texts, signs and content. In addition, Barthes seeks to understand the construction of a way of life via the structuring and interpretation of meanings. In the meanings of texts and practices, and in the reproduction of meanings undertaken by audiences, individuals and groups can be understood to negotiate identities. In Barthes's work, cultural theory is concerned to ask questions about those conflicts and ideologies which shape a way of life but which often go unnoticed or unanalysed. Media and cultural signs, then, are not to be taken for granted.

We can develop Barthes's work a little further in relation to how signs work. For instance, when the news media use shots of the White House to depict the United States, or transmit pictures of the Union Flag flying over Buckingham Palace in order to signify Britain, these image concentrations can often paper over political and cultural conflicts. Thus, an image powerfully contains and homogenises what in reality is far more disparate than the single image implies. Barthes's analysis of culture is one which focuses on the placing and structure of signs in cultural life and media output. Barthes uses examples from the field of visual media and visual cultures, but he also works with language. Drawing on and expanding work in the field of de Saussure and structuralism, Barthes examines popular media through the theoretical perspective of semiotics (theory of signs and sign systems). He shows how

a sign operates at the level of *denotation* (primary signification) and *connotation* (secondary signification). For instance,
the *signifier* 'cat', operating at the level of denotation, signi-
fies a feline mammal. However, this sign, now working at the
level of connotation, produces a secondary signification 'cat'.
This second meaning can be used to signify 'slinky', 'subtle',
'graceful' or 'person regarded as sly or stealthy'.

In terms of cultural analysis, Barthes's work is very useful
indeed. First, he argues that all signs in culture work on two
levels: denotation and connotation. Secondly, all culture, in
Barthes's account, is composed of sign systems which are 'pol-
ysemic'. By this, he means that all signs contain far more than
the meaning which operates at the level of denotation (as in the
example 'cat' above). Thirdly, media output, because it draws
on and exploits this plurality of meaning, is necessarily
involved in activities which are never far from a society's myths
and ideologies. For Barthes, cultural theory and analysis are the
means of laying bare or exposing that body of ideas and beliefs
which seems to operate in the interests of the dominant cultural
group. Here is an extract from one of his most well-cited discussions of the popular French magazine *Paris Match*.

> I am at the barber's, and a copy of *Paris Match* is offered to me.
> On the cover, a young Negro in a French uniform is saluting, with
> his eyes uplifted, probably fixed on the . . . tricolour [French flag].
> But . . . I see very well what it signifies to me: that France is a great
> Empire, that all her sons, without colour discrimination, faithfully
> serve under her flag, and that there is no better answer to the
> detractors of an alleged colonialism than the zeal shown by this
> Negro in serving his so-called oppressors. I am therefore faced
> with a greater semiological system: there is a signifier. . . (a black
> solider giving the French salute); [and] there is a signified (it is a
> purposeful mixture of Frenchness and militariness). (125–6)

Barthes's work enables us to see that cultural theory and
analysis entails:

1. Watching, looking at, listening to and reading media
   output in terms of its signs, words, images, etc.

2. Barthes's model contends that the critical examination and
   textual analysis of culture will be concerned on one level
   with its representations (what we see or hear) and the ways
   in which something is represented (how the sound or
   image is put together for consumption). Barthes writes
   much about the cultural production of the voice, the body
   and the face. In an essay on the faces of celebrities and
   gender, he analyses facial expressions, the significance of
   skin colour, the subject's way of looking and gazing, and
   the social context in which the subject is situated.

3. Barthes draws attention to media sign systems and
   common-sense discussions about cultural meaning. For
   example, what does 'solider' mean in the light of French
   history and imperialism? What does the picture of a black
   soldier on the front of a popular magazine suggest about
   cultural change in France during the 1950s? For Barthes,
   cultural analysis aims to uncover the relations between
   political ideology, power (represented (in the magazine) in
   terms of French colonialism) and nationhood (or the
   media's construction of 'Frenchness'). Frenchness is not
   something which pre-exists its representation, but is produced and consumed in relation to the magazine.

ENCODING – PROGRAMME DISCOURSE – DECODING: STUART HALL

Earlier chapters in Part II have stressed the importance of production and consumption in the theory and study of culture.
The relations between production, output, consumption and
identity have been central to the research and analysis of the
media and culture industries over the last twenty years. In
many ways, Hall's 'Encoding and Decoding in the Television
Discourse' (Hall, Hobson, Lowe and Willis, 1992) contains
many of the principal elements which were later enlarged and
expanded on in the work of media theorist David Morley in the
1970s and 1980s, and more recent work. Two key textbooks

which will be on most reading lists in cultural theory modules are *Representation: Cultural Representations and Signifying Practices* (1997; ed. Stuart Hall) and *Doing Cultural Studies: The Story of the Sony Walkman* (1997; eds du Gay, Hall, Janes, Mackay and Negus). They are particularly useful in the theorisation and analysis of cultural production and consumption.

However, Hall's earlier encoding and decoding model continues to prove useful when undertaking cultural analysis. His essay shows how television programmes (for example, the news) can be understood initially in terms of two axes: 'encoding and meaning structures A'; and 'decoding and meaning structures B'. It can be presented as follows:

TV programme made into discourse

Production/encoding   Consumption/decoding

<u>*Encoding*</u>: *meaning structures A*   <u>*Encoding*</u>: *meaning structures B*

Domains of knowledge
Domains of production
Domains of technical

Consider the situation of a TV news journalist whose job it is to (re)present and report a political crisis or major event. The first element to note in a cultural analysis pursuing Hall's model is that no event (for example, death of world leader, or anti-globalisation rally) happens 'raw' or untouched by the forms, systems and technologies of media representation. While the report might seem transparent, or free of discourses and ideology, closer analysis exposes its mediated and constructed status.

To produce a meaningful piece of news or an intelligible report, the production teams work on the basis of existing meanings and ideas, both about how to make news and how news is decoded by viewers. Media production (encoding) is framed by 'knowledge-in-use concerning the routines of production, historically defined technical skills, professional ideologies, institutional knowledges, definitions and assumptions, [and] assumptions about the audience' (Hall et al., 1992: 129). For Hall, no event makes sense outside the terms which manufacture or encode the event into a meaningful discourse. This 'making' of the news, alongside its 're-presentation' makes the task of media analysis all the more important.

A number of critical questions has been raised about the extent of the media's influence in determining how audiences think in relation to the events being represented. Critics and cultural theorists have pointed to the effects of the media in relation to group behaviour, cross-cultural relations, globalisation and political power. Does the news, then, determine how audiences think about a specific situation? In addition, how does decoding operate, and are audiences in a position to decode the media as they choose? In like manner to Barthes, so Hall draws attention to the ideological, political and contextual dimensions of the encoded text.

Encoded texts are ultimately decoded by audiences. But Hall shows how an event is made into a discourse, given a particular meaning, framed within a televisual shape and subjected to frequent editing. Thus, although the moment of audience decoding is the third part of the model, a second element of Hall's model is the programme discourse itself. In a sense, this is the point at which mediation takes place. Although an event has its own three-dimensional and 'factual' reality, another discursive fact – Hall's second part of the model – has to be taken into account. In the work of Hall and others, reality exists regardless of language, but reality is nonetheless mediated by and through language as well as the discourses of language. What Hall means by discourse is the way language invariably makes sense in relation to cultural and social codes such as, for instance, the discourses of gender, race and ethnicity or social class. It is the TV programme and its status as mediated meaningful discourse which is the object of the audience's decoding. But it is the tripartite alliance of encoding, TV discourse and decoding which is the key element in Hall's model and in cultural analysis.

Dominant, negotiated and resistant cultures

Hall's own complication of the above model makes it useful for media analysis today. He discusses how each element in the encoding/decoding process is beset by other factors. What programme makers intend to say or represent, for instance, is not necessarily obvious to audiences. Moreover, audiences differ as to the decoding and meaning of the same programme, something brought to light in David Morley's analysis of the media. Hall suggests that at least three positions of decoding can be adopted by audiences. The first, known as the 'dominant-hegemonic position', is one in which audiences operate within society's dominant code. David Morley (1980) shows how audiences decoded the reporting of the release of a prisoner in terms of 'personal drama' rather than in terms of 'the political background' or the wider 'political implications' of the case.

The second decoding position is one which is negotiated – one which Hall thinks is adopted by the majority. This kind of media analysis will examine how audiences work with a mixture of adaptive and oppositional elements. The position of negotiation is fraught with contradictions in that the television discourse does and does not provide an accurate encoding of the event or situation. In a sense, Hall is pointing out how all decoding of media discourse is fraught with ambiguities of which the media text is itself never immune. However, when decoding takes place on the basis of Hall's third position, the 'oppositional' perspective, then the media message is being subjected to decodings which attempt to close down the text's plural meanings. Hall uses the example of a viewer who listens to a discussion which proposes the need to limit wages. Every mention of 'national interest' during the broadcast is read or decoded as 'class interest'.

Circuit of culture

Pivotal in the work of Barthes, Hall and a number of other cultural theorists is language, and the key feature of language is its function as a 'representational system'. Language and the work of representation are central in the final framework we will examine in this section. In many senses it is a fairly straightforward model, and it is a key part of the Open University's series of introductory textbooks in cultural and media studies. The circuit of culture applies five key terms in its mapping and analysis of the relations between culture and the economy. A useful way of outlining this model is to summarise the key propositions put forward in *Doing Cultural Studies: The Story of the Sony Walkman* (Du Gay et al., 1997). In discussing the production and consumption of the Walkman, the editors show how this cultural artefact can be understood in relation to the five interrelated concepts of the circuit:

1. Representation: all cultural artefacts, whilst they have to be 'produced', have, in capitalist economies, also to be represented. Although the argument is more complex than is summarised here, we can see that the Sony Walkman had to be represented or advertised in order to be sold. Thus, representation is one of the key elements in understanding all cultures in that people are forced to use systems of representation in order to communicate with each other.

2. Identity: representations make sense in relation to people and identities. The Sony Walkman is a device whose principal function concerns the playing of and listening to music. Using earphones, the Walkman can be listened to in very public and private ways at the same time. However, the Walkman was advertised and marketed as an artefact associated with youth, 'rebelliousness' and independence. The Walkman device can, of course, be purchased and used by anyone. However, by linking the Walkman to a particular identity, Sony is able to consolidate its own identity as one which is up to date and forward looking.

3. Production: here, production means not only the materials and technology which combine to make the Walkman. Rather, the Walkman also has to be culturally produced, or made to mean something in relation to the identity of

the target group of consumers. The users of the Walkman, then, produce particular forms of identification which confirm and exceed Sony's expectations.

4. Consumption: in making the Walkman signify initially in relation to youth identities, so the Sony Corporation establish a link between the object and its intended consumers. However, the consumption of the object happens in at least two ways. First, the Walkman is bought to be consumed as a personal stereo device. Secondly, it is consumed in relation to social and cultural identity. Alternatively phrased, the Walkman has a 'use' value which serves a specific purpose, and it has an 'exchange' value whose meanings exceed those articulated at the level of actual use.

5. Regulation: not long after the Walkman was introduced, marketed and sold to capitalist economies in the West, it became increasingly clear that it was something which was being marketed in relation to the articulation of specific identities. However, the device was used in ways which challenged the distinctions between public and private space. This blurring of boundaries meant that the Walkman had to be regulated (for example, it can only be used according to certain conventions or in controlled situations). There is nothing unusual about the regulation of cultural artefacts. However, the theoretical framework links regulation to all the other elements in the circuit of culture. Regulation, then, is concerned with the regulation of behaviours and identities, and not simply the activity of listening to music using a personal stereo.

We have seen that language and representation are understood in relation to the notion of texts and cultural artefacts. It is to be recalled, however, that Barthes's discussion of the myths which structure contemporary mass culture proposes that textual representations are neither natural nor neutral. His work demonstrates how signs and texts are caught up in a history whose apparent inevitability is attributable not to an uncontrollable nature but to the force fields of myth and ideology. Analyses which attend to the political economy of media and culture, alongside those which attend to issues such as cultural consumption and meaning, demonstrate the continuing importance of quantitative and qualitative investigations in cultural research. But all theories and frameworks in the analysis of the construction and representation of culture make more complete sense when set against the backdrop of the political and economic contexts in which all media output is produced.

FURTHER READING

Barthes, R. (1973), *Mythologies*, London: Jonathan Cape.

Du Gay, P., Hall, S., Janes, L., Mackay, H. and Negus, K. (1997), *Doing Cultural Studies: The Story of the Sony Walkman*, London: Sage.

Hall, S. (ed.) (1997), *Representation: Cultural Representations and Signifying Practices*, London: Sage.

Hall, S., Hobson, D., Lowe, A. and Willis, P. (1992 (1980)), *Culture, Media, Language*, London: Routledge.

Hermes, J. (1995), *Reading Women's Magazines*, Cambridge: Polity.

Jenkins, H. (1992), *Textual Poachers*, New York: Routledge.

Morley, D. (1980), *The 'Nationwide' Audience*, London: BFI.

Radway, J. (1987), *Reading the Romance: Women, Patriarchy, and Popular literature*, London: Verso.

Thornham, S. and Purvis, T. (2004), *Television Drama: Theories and Identities*, Basingstoke: Palgrave Macmillan.

PART III
Study Skills

12 WEEK ONE, SEMESTER I, LEVEL I

STRUCTURES OF SUPPORT

Modules, module outlines and module guides

In the first few weeks of university, it is vital to know what you are doing, whom to contact if in doubt, and to establish good study and research habits from the start. This section of the book, then, is concerned with helping you to 'learn how to learn'. University degree programmes are all the more interesting and enjoyable if you are prepared to ask questions, engage with the reading and research, and adopt a critical and interrogative approach to learning. In many ways, this section of the book cannot underline enough the importance of critique and critical inquiry.

In order to facilitate processes more smoothly, universities have in place all sorts of support systems and structures. In the first few weeks, and especially during the induction sessions, it is important that you:

1. Get a copy of the module outline forms or module guidebooks (see below) and/or the degree handbook. The handbook is very general and provides key details of options you can choose over three years. The module handbook is more detailed and plays a much more significant role in your research and studies on a day-to-day basis. These are vital sources of information and are sometimes available on faculty websites or issued as hard copies in induction meetings.

2. Find out where the faculty or departmental notice board is located. Key details about changes to the programme or

names of tutors are often listed here. Online notice boards are also common, as are the posting of details via emails.

3. Sort an email account (either one you use already or a university account).

4. Make sure you know where the school office is, who your personal tutor is, and what the procedures are for tutorial meetings.

5. Join the library!

6. Find out where the learning resource centre is located (often referred to as LRC). This is the place where students often submit essays and receive receipts for submitted work.

7. Find out if there are any charges for modules (for example, some media production modules ask students to pay a small fee for use of materials and some equipment).

8. Make sure you know about computing facilities.

9. Get to know other people on the course.

10. Have at least one meeting with your personal tutor within the first month of being at university.

Modules
Part I of this book provides an account of how modules contribute to the degree programme. To summarise briefly:

1. Most degree programmes will take three or four years to complete.

2. Each year, you will usually study modules of 10, 20 or 30 credits.

3. Each year the credits will amount to 120 credits (a total of 360 for three years).

In the first year of study, students are often confused about where classes take place, how often seminars occur, whom to ask for an extension to an essay deadline, what the key reading is and so on. The module itself will be arranged round lecturers and seminars, production classes and workshops, one-to-one meetings and independent study. The module will always be accompanied by TWO documents, the module outline form, and the module guide or handbook. They are worth reading in some detail.

Module outline forms

A module outline or module summary provides students with key information about the module. Sometimes the information is online, part of the module guide or issued in the first taught session.

Module outlines provide key data for students and the faculty (school or department) in which the module is taught. This kind of information is included on front covers of assignments so that it is clear to administration staff which essay is being assessed, by whom and for which module. The learning outcomes indicate what the module hopes to achieve in relation to teaching and learning.

Example: module outline

Module Title: Recent Television Genres

MODULE CODE	MED 147
CREDITS	20
LEVEL	1
FACULTY	Humanities and Social Sciences
MODULE BOARD	Media
PREREQUISITES	None
CO-REQUISITES	None
TEACHING HOURS	200 of which 80 are contact based around lectures and seminars.

Learning outcomes
Upon successful completion of this module, students will:
1. Show knowledge of a wide range of television genres and working practices.

2. Demonstrate a critical knowledge of genre and media theory in television studies.
3. Use and apply this knowledge in evaluative ways in the analysis of television output and texts.
4. Present arguments about television in written and spoken forms.
5. Demonstrate skills of written and spoken presentation.

Module synopsis

This module investigates television and television output. It focuses on the analysis of recent television genres. During the course of this module you will be encouraged additionally to consider a variety of different approaches to analysing popular television programmes. It is important while taking this module that you watch television, read about television, question television and consider its relation to other media. Examples of British, Asian and European output will be studied.

Approaches to learning and teaching

Lectures, seminars, group discussions, presentations, question–answer
Lectures: 12 @ 1-hour lectures; 12 @ 2-hour seminars.
Assessment methods
Essay: 2k words 80%
Presentation: 15 minutes: 20%
All learning outcomes are assessed.

Indicative Reading

Books and sources will be listed here.
Staff
The tutors for this module will be listed here.

You can see why the module outline form provides important data. The outline provided here is a very simplified, student-friendly version of what can sometimes be quite a complex document. All degree programmes will have copies of module outlines for every module and if you want to know more about a module before starting the course, then perhaps ask if they are available. Some universities will provide 'student' synopses or have material available on web pages. The learning outcomes are always worth thinking about because they indicate how students are being assessed. Essays or examinations will be assessed in relation to learning outcomes, and so always have them in view when researching for an assignment. The reading list similarly provides key information serving as a general guide as to who is publishing and researching in the field of study. And the content synopsis provides in summary form the rationale of the module.

Module guides and handbooks

The module guide is one of the key documents of any module. The example used here intentionally reiterates some of the topics and study skills discussed in this book and reflects fairly accurately how study skills are taught on the first year of a degree programme in media and cultural studies.

The importance of the module guide cannot be underestimated.

1. It provides key data about the module.

2. It is often available on web pages.

3. It lists how students are assessed.

4. It contains details of assessment criteria and dates for submissions.

TIME MANAGEMENT

Time management is never straightforward. It is not easy in the first year of study to work out exactly how much time is needed for production projects, essays, seminar presentations, group work or diaries and portfolios. Moreover, students come from different contexts, have different needs and demands. However, a number of points can be made about the importance of managing time and responsibilities.

Table 12.1 Example of a module guide

Degree Programme: Media and Cultural Studies
Module Title: Study and Research Methods
Module Code: 135
Credit Value: 20
Session: 2004–2005
Class Time: Mondays 14.00–16.00hrs
Module Leader: Name

Programme

Week	Themes and Issues
1	Introduction: why 'study skills'; audit of existing skills; setting goals; reviewing progress: general introductions. Valuing the contributions of other group members. Reviewing what you do each week: end-of-session review introduced. Reading for week 1: listed here.
2	Organisation and time management: organisation of day/week/month; working to deadlines; structuring study and reading; structuring study for work and leisure. Action plans and progress files. Reading for week 2: listed here.
3	What is research? Research skills and note-taking. Keeping notes; using notes; using PC/WP for notes. Experience so far of research. What individuals have done in relation to research demands of current modules. Using resources for research. Qualitative and quantitative research. Reading for week 3: listed here.
4	Reading and structuring reading. Making notes from reading. Records/log of reading activities. What we do with reading; no writing essays without reading texts. How to record bibliographic details: some conventions and practices. Primary and secondary sources: key works in subject field alongside student textbooks and guidebooks about primary research. Adopting critical approaches to reading and study. Reading for week 4: listed here
5/6	Conventions of academic writing: structuring the academic essay; writing and form (for example, evaluative, descriptive, critical, etc.); comparing different types of texts (for example, essays compared to newspaper reports; sports reports as opposed to writing about sports; etc.). Plagiarism. Reading for week 5/6: listed here Reading Week
7	Practical modules: report writing and working with audiences:

and follow-up exercises for later seminars: joint session with all 135 seminar groups; details of venue and time to follow.
Reading for week 7: listed here

8   Introducing spoken/group presentation skills: working on group presentations; team working; key points when doing short spoken presentations.
Reading for week 8: listed here.

9   Library skills, literature searches and information retrieval: (in library) details to be announced in each seminar group. Feel free to ask library staff questions or raise issues on the basis of your experience of using the library so far in your degree studies.
Reading for week 9: listed here.

10   Assessment and analysis: examining previous work for 135; (2) action plan (using either your own report from practical module or your own essay from any module). In reviews for this week, list ALL the strengths and weaknesses of your own chosen piece of work (for example, essay from last semester) and outline a short action plan on improvements. These can be listed in progress files.
Reading for week 10: listed here.

11   Working in media production: skills and abilities in the use of media equipment, working according to industry codes and regulations, and working in teams where decisions reflect individual initiative as well as group efforts.
Media ethics, equal opportunities, and media policy and law.
Reading for week 11: listed here.

12   Presentations. Brief: Audience: prospective students of media and cultural studies. Task: you will present a discussion accompanied by a short group report which outlines the value of media and cultural studies degrees to the wider society. Work in groups of 4 and present issues to rest of the group. Your presentation notes to be used in review for this week.

13   One-to-one essay tutorials as required. Brief: how have study and research skills been incorporated into your studies for degree modules this semester? You are encouraged to use key headings from media employability documents to structure your discussion.

14   Reviews and evaluations: summary of what to expect in Level II Research Methods.

Assessment schedule
All coursework should be submitted to the office in the Faculty of Media. Assignments submitted after the deadline of DATE will be awarded zero except in mitigating circumstances supported by relevant

Table 12.1 Continued

documentation (such as a GP's letter or note from your personal tutor).

If you think you might have problems completing or submitting an assignment please contact me, the Module Leader, to discuss the situation.

Assessment Components
Essay (written): 35%
Question: how have study and research skills been incorporated into your degree modules this semester? You are encouraged to use key headings from media employability documents to structure your discussion.

The essay should be 2k words and written according to academic conventions addressed in the module. TWO copies of the essay should be submitted. The criteria for the assessment of the essay can be found on-line on the school web page.

Group Presentation (spoken presentation): 35%
Audience: prospective students of media and cultural studies. Task: you will present a discussion accompanied by a short group report which outlines the value of media and cultural studies degrees to the wider society. Each group will present their findings to all members of the module. The presentation should be based on your research, your findings and recommendations. The group presentation should allow students to reflect critically on experiences of media practices, media theory and criticism, and media working environments.

Progress File: 30%
Using the format provided (a copy in module guides and also on web pages) you should log and discuss details of skills and your personal development and progress during this module. This should be completed on a weekly basis and the Peer Assessment for Group Work must be completed at the end of the module and submitted with the Progress File. Templates for the Progress File and copies of the Peer Assessment for Group Work are available from the office.

Practical measures

1. Work out the best time for study. If there is one period in the day when output is greater, then this is worth exploiting to the full.

2. Decide on places for study. Production projects are not usually undertaken in libraries, whereas essay and seminar preparation may be centred around the library. Some

students find it easier to work from home, or in parts of the library which are not silent-study areas. Some students work better with others around, and prefer to talk through the drafting process or as ideas crystallise.

3. In addition, write out a weekly or monthly schedule, based around the timetable for the semester. Note down when taught sessions are and plan time around them for study, research, leisure, etc. A monthly schedule is a great way of establishing good time management practices at the start of the degree.

4. It is sensible if not essential to keep the weekend free if this is the least productive time of the week for reading and research.

5. Time spent reading through lecture notes after lectures means key ideas can be recalled with ease. Some students word process lecture notes as an additional way of establishing a knowledge base which can be added to with relative ease.

6. Be realistic about how much can be achieved in a set time period.

7. A really productive use of time is to identify at the outset what it is that will be achieved.

8. The credit size of the module (for example, 10, 20 or 30 credits) will determine how much time you will want to allocate to study and research.

Critical frames

Attitudes and approaches to study are important in the early stages of studying for a degree. It is vital to approach the task in hand critically. ALL work is important at university and so time is never wasted in the long term. Adopting a critical frame of mind, alongside a belief in the value of the work you do, always makes the time spent on assignments seem worthwhile.

Preparations

For some pieces of work it seems that much time is spent achieving very little. This is an experience which all students have at some point, and not just those starting degree courses. It is really important, therefore, to start all work well in advance of the deadline date for submission, and, if others are involved, make sure agreement is reached as to dates for completion.

Drafting

Drafting work in the early stages of a degree can take more time than in second or third years. However, the time it takes to draft and redraft (whether this is essays or production projects) is time that is well spent and it is a skill that is usefully deployed in other situations.

Long-term and short-term goals

Thinking of time management in terms of goals is one way of maximising output. Some work requires much greater input and effort (for example, the dissertation or extended production project). Establish the short-term goals of the project and the long-term goals, and stick to the schedule.

13 READING, WRITING AND ESSAYS

This chapter deals in detail with academic writing. Essays, extended pieces of writing, dissertations, reports and executive summaries for production projects are among the most common ways of being assessed at university. Many media and cultural studies degree courses use essays as part of the continuous assessment of the student. On a number of degree programmes, essays are in fact the principal method of assessing students' work. Often the essay is attached to module credits as follows:

10 credit module: 2.5k word essay.

20 credit module: 3.5–4.5k word essay.

20 credit module: 2k word essay (50%) and seminar presentation (50%).

30 credit or dissertation module: 8–10k words.

Clearly, other methods of assessment are used (examinations, presentations, production-based work, etc.), though the summary above is one which reflects many of the assessment practices in UK universities.

WHAT IS AN ESSAY?

An essay presents an argument and systematically discusses a series of connected points specifically in relation to a question. The essay, in responding to the question, will present and argue its position in a continuous and coherent way. Structured around key paragraphs, each of which introduces, develops and anticipates the following point, the essay should always cohere around the question being answered. The main body of the essay should be introduced appropriately and should be followed by paragraphs which regularly signal to the reader the essay's direction, its underpinning logic and its use of evidence and/or theory. The essay should be concluded by paragraphs which amplify the points already raised. Introductions should only introduce what is in the essay, and conclusions should not introduce substantially new material. Finally, the essay should conform to agreed standards and academic conventions. The essay, which should be word-processed, should always be referenced according to bibliographic conventions.

Important points

1. In the introduction refer only to what is in the body of the essay or raise points which might be relevant to the body of the essay.

2. Structure the essay around a body of paragraphs which introduce a key point, discuss the key point, provisionally conclude the key point and signal what to expect in the succeeding paragraph.

3. Adopt a specific approach in your arguments (for example, for and against, compare and contrast, on the one hand, on the other hand, thesis, antithesis, synthesis, and so on).

4. Conclude your essay only on the basis of what has been raised in the essay and only amplify what has been already discussed.

Critical reflection

The chances are that most of you will be familiar with the above structure. In many ways, the most demanding part of writing an essay is the preparation and critical reflection. A number of stages is involved in writing the essay (or dissertation). Among the most important initial stages are selecting the question, followed by the extensive reading (depending on the type of question you are answering) and critical thinking. In this context, 'thinking' means understanding the question and making sure you have considered the angles from which the question can be approached. Thinking is also concerned with trying to adopt critical and reflective perspectives. If you manage your time, there is no need to rush into the writing of the essay. Strike a balance in an ongoing process which involves writing, thinking, revising and rewriting, and then rethinking, reviewing and so on until the piece is ready.

Reading and research

There are lots of short guides which tell students how to write essays, and these are valuable in any student's library. However, one of the most important tasks is reading, both widely and critically. Students who repeatedly perform well in essays will have read round the topic, and this reading is evidenced in a well-researched and informed argument. But good essays always show the extent to which the student has engaged critically with the material, demonstrating awareness of different points of view, and possibly coming down on one side of a problem more than others.

Whilst it is important to write an essay which is balanced, this does not mean that the essay cannot finally establish which position is the preferred one. This is especially the case for extended essays, dissertations and work undertaken at level II and level III. However, essays which are able to discuss issues in reflective, evaluative and critical ways are essays which were started well in advance of the deadline for submission. Such essays will also demonstrate the time the student has spent reading, researching, thinking, grasping, deciding upon and finally arguing a particular position. Always remember that what you write is valuable: it is something you have spent time doing, and it is valuable because, in its own way, it contributes to the increasingly refined and interesting ways undergraduate essays make comments on the media, culture and society.

Preparing and drafting and writing: ten-point plan

Plans only work if you are prepared to make them work! But plans can also be revised on the basis of good practice and reflection. Here is one which might work for you.

1. Look at the questions, and choose one which best suits your interests and strengths.

2. Make sure the question is chosen well in advance of the time for submission.

3. Make sure adequate research time and drafting time is built into each day or every two to three days.

4. Begin amassing ideas, books, sources, evidence and material which will contribute to a good essay. Put photocopied material, drafts and cuttings into an essay folder and gradually select material which is most relevant to the essay.

5. Start writing whenever key ideas emerge or when arguments are beginning to form. When note-making from books or articles, make sure you word-process from the start, adding your own critical comments as you write.

6. Begin to order notes and ideas, and try to imagine the structure of the essay.

7. Review notes and begin to structure key parts of the essay into paragraphs, and try to gauge the overall structure of the essay.

8. Paragraphs should present a key point or idea, should support the idea with evidence (for example, for and against), should make the point and begin to introduce the point which is to be discussed in the next paragraph.

9. Begin to put these paragraphs together into a structure which has a strong sense of the body of the essay. The body of the essay should be about 65–75 per cent of the essay with the remaining 25–35 per cent given over to introduction and conclusion. The introduction and conclusion are the last things to write. An essay can only be concluded on the basis of what has been said, and an introduction cannot introduce something which does not exist already.

10. Write the final draft of the essay at least three days before submission, and read the essay again two days before submission and consider any changes or improvements.

The above plan for writing essays will work for some students and not others. In a sense, each student finds her or his own way and usually sticks with that method until another one supersedes it.

Essay writing: further details

The writing of the essay or dissertation does not start with the introduction. That might seem odd. The essay has to start somewhere, and the essay or dissertation has to have an introduction. However, an introduction can't be written until the essay writer finally knows what to introduce. Moreover, introductions are not to be confused with the aims and objectives of the essay. It is possible to start writing the essay or dissertation with a very clear sense of focus, and with a very clear sense of aim, yet still leave the introduction till the final stages. Introductions, then, are probably the last part of the essay to be written. This does not mean that an introduction is not imagined from the outset of writing the essay. And it does not mean that the drafting and planning is without structure, aim or purpose. Key ideas need to be thought through from the start. But an essay takes shape before an introduction does. Collect the evidence and think through the ideas; comment on the evidence, in critical and reflective ways; make evaluations and judgements where you can; and begin to get a sense of the body of the essay. These kinds of activities precede the writing of the introduction and conclusion.

Tackling the question: critical approaches

Below is an essay in 'note' form. The essay question is in italics and underlined.

1. Read the essay title.

2. Consider some of the issues that emerge as you think through the question – whether you are familiar with the topic or not. If it helps, jot down your own thoughts and compare them with the suggestions here.

3. Then read through the points raised below the essay question.

With reference to contemporary examples, critically discuss how far advertising and advertisements allow consumers to 'identity shop'.

It is important to think critically about the question in order to provide a judicious and informed argument. We can consider some of the ways of tackling this question in relation to criticality.

1. The first activity is to read the question quite a few times in order to get a sense of its nuances and its different ways of being interpreted. Consider discussing the question with a fellow student.

2. Begin to note the wording. 'With reference to . . .' means that the question expects students to give examples, and so essays which don't respond in that way are limited from the start.

3. The question asks students to 'critically discuss'. The word 'discuss' is fairly broad and leaves open a range of responses: there is more than one way to discuss something (see later discussion of examinations). The use of the word 'critically', however, is important and it is the essay's way of encouraging students to engage in some of the controversial issues which the question might raise. Other words could be used in questions. *Assess, consider* and *examine* are some of the typical ways of asking students questions in essays. Note that these words are very different to *describe, outline, summarise*. The latter set includes words which require different kinds of responses, and do not usually require vast amounts of detail. But they may precede the key stem of the question (as in *'Outline what is meant by identity and critically examine . . . '*). (See Chapter 15, 'Examinations').

4. When questions ask 'how far' or 'to what extent', it implies that the question can be answered in at least TWO ways. Advertisements either do not allow consumers to identity shop, or advertisements do allow consumers to identity shop. Within these two extremes, there are clearly a range of other possibilities and the essay is asking students to address those extremes. Essays will give examples of how far advertising does what the question suggests (a lot, not very much, equally balanced, or more ambiguous (in some cases 'yes' but in other cases 'no')).

5. 'Consumers' is a fairly specific (and, for some, a fairly contentious) term, and answers will initially make direct references to the identity of the consumer. It may be that answers seek to specify in more exact ways what sort of consumers the essay writer will focus on in the response. The term is also contentious in that 'consumers' assumes much about the society in which consumer identities matter. The terms which the essay uses will always be referred to in answers.

6. 'Identity shop' is surrounded by inverted commas. This is the question's way of making students aware of a specific

language and discourse. Essays which don't address this key phrase might be more limited than those which directly confront the key words.

Criticality and critique

Critical thinking is not to be confused with being negative or pessimistic. Two other words associated with critical are 'critic' and 'criticise', both of which suggest a tradition where criticism is either unconstructive and unhelpful, or deeply personal and subjective. Another word associated with critical – 'critique' – provides a sharper sense of what it means to act critically in relation to reading and writing. Critique and critical thinking occur when – on the basis of reading, reflection, evaluation and discussion – students are able to make judgements about ideas in analytic and measured ways. An approach to study and reading which is marked by a sense of critique or critical analysis takes time to develop and so don't be disheartened or discouraged, and always value the work you do.

Don't think that being analytical means essays are dispassionate. Similarly, a 'measured' response does not mean essays have to steer a middle ground or sit on the fence. It might mean, however, that you adopt a specific method, theory or approach which allows a topic or object to be viewed in one light more than another. This kind of thinking and writing is to be encouraged as it usually means some engagement with the material has taken place. Critical thinking in media and cultural studies might entail thinking against the grain of an argument, and assessing competing positions and views. None of the subjects and disciplines taught in universities provide one way of examining or critiquing a problem, and media and cultural studies degrees are no exception.

For example, it is often suggested that some television output contributes to increased violence in society, or that broadcasting standards are lower than they were thirty years ago, or that the news media are controlled by a small, unelected and undemocratic minority. Watching popular television, holidaying with package companies or listening to popular music are thought by some critics not to require as high a level of cognitive, intellectual or aesthetic discrimination as going to see a performance of *King Lear* at the local theatre, visiting an art gallery to see the latest installation piece or buying a recording of Gregorian chant. Some people in media and cultural studies adopt quantitative approaches to analyse these issues whereas others pursue qualitative research. Thinking critically about these claims means probing the claims and the assumptions which underpin the claims. This will entail using evidence and reading others' research in order to make a more informed, a more considered and a less subjective judgement.

Approaches to working critically

Consider the claims that are made about the media and culture:

- Hollywood films are rubbish.

- Soap operas are cheap, formulaic dramas made for uncritical and unthinking audiences.

- There's a world of difference between a popular women's romance and a novel by George Eliot.

- We don't honour actors anymore, only C-grade celebrities.

- Nobody speaks English correctly these days.

- The media manipulates us and forces us to do things we wouldn't normally do.

Imagine these have been set as essay questions, as discussion topics for a seminar or as part of a presentation where the group is required to examine the validity of the claims. Ask:

1. What is the context of the claims?
2. Who is making the claims?

3. What research is available which examines the field or topic?

4. If it is possible to agree with the claim, and if so, to what extent: mostly agree, mostly disagree, somewhere in the middle?

Working critically with essays
We can consider approaches to working critically if we return to the essay question introduced earlier.

Reminder: *With reference to contemporary examples, critically discuss how far advertising and advertisements allow consumers to 'identity shop'.*

1. Always think through the terms and references of the claim; never assume the statement or question is there to be agreed with and always establish an agenda.

2. Ensure that identity is seen in complex terms. Although 'identity' is an important term, it is always more than one thing (for example, gender, sexuality, social class, ethnicity and so on).

3. Decide which specific aspects of identity will be considered. Use broad as well as specific references in order to establish well-rounded responses.

4. Make clear that identity can be seen in terms of something given (we can't take away the location of one's birth), as well as something social (we make sense to each other in relation to the society of birth or socialisation). But identity is something which is in part determined and in part negotiated.

5. Ensure that identity is seen in relation to the texts and advertisements which promote senses of identity – but don't think that the text will then give consumers an identity: consumption is active, not passive, but advertisements nonetheless remain powerful shapers of choice; texts are marked by

multiple discourses and we read them in multiple contexts, but, in the final analysis, consumption involves monetary exchange at some point.

6. Think again about the phrase 'identity shop'. Does 'shop' mean 'buy' or does it mean 'consume'? Does 'shop' mean we can go looking for an identity in the way that we can go to the shops to look at products rather than buy them? To buy a CD or car is not to consume the object; and to shop at one store as opposed to another is as much a cultural as it is an economic activity.

7. The question asks you to think about advertisements and identities. Remember that an advertisement is a text, and texts always assume readers. The answer to the question, then, will want to consider the two-way processes in the making of meaning. However, another question emerges: Does the advertisement make consumers shop, or do the consumers want to shop regardless of the advertisement? We can't say that advertisements will position us exactly (as young, as old, as students, as thirty-something, etc.), even though there is a dominant reading (this advertisement seems to speak to 'me'). Consumers will produce other readings and rereadings of advertising texts.

THE HARVARD REFERENCING SYSTEM: A SUMMARY

All written work at university, but especially essays and dissertations, will make reference to and cite the work of others. Quoting references shows your attempts to understand the work of others, and critically incorporate it into your essay. It is important, therefore, to be both consistent and accurate.

Citation in the text: author/date method

All 'evidence' which is taken from the work of another must be cited. This is the case whether you are quoting the work directly, paraphrasing or summarising it. If you use the Harvard System, you will cite publications in the essay by using the author's surname and the year of publication in one of the forms shown below.

Here are a few examples of how this is done:

1. In a popular study, Hall (1973, p. 76) contended that . . .

2. More controversial studies (e.g. Hennessy, 2000) argue that . . .

3. Hall (1994a) suggests that . . . (The 'a' refers to one of two publications by Hall in 1994; hence 1994b and so on.)

4. Thornham and Purvis (2005) make clear that . . . (For a publication with two authors, both surnames are used.)

5. du Gay et al. (1997) have argued . . . (The 'et al.' is used when there are more than two authors for a publication.)

6. A study by Hall (1973, cited in Davis, 2004) . . . (This makes clear that the source for the Hall evidence is in Davis and not Hall.)

Page numbers and quotations

1. It is not necessary to use page numbers if you are discussing the argument of a book in general terms. For example, 'Hall's work (DATE) allows us to see that . . .'

2. When you are making reference to a specific point within a book or article, then you must give the page numbers (for example, Author, 1990: 56–7).

3. When you are quoting material of less than perhaps forty words, then this will be included in the body of the text using quotation marks.

4. When you are quoting material of substantially more than forty words, then the quotation will be indented, it will start

on a new line, it will not use quotation marks, and the page number will be included in parentheses after the quote.

5. Charts, tables and diagrams should be referenced as though they were a quotation.

SOURCES AND BIBLIOGRAPHY

1. The bibliography will come at the end of the essay or dissertation. It lists all the references (and not simply quotations!) to cited documents in the final piece of written work.

2. If you use the Harvard System, then the references will be listed in alphabetical order of authors' surnames.

3. If you have cited more than one source by the same author, they should be listed chronologically (earliest first), and then by letter in the case of the same year (2000a, 2000b).

4. The elements of a bibliographical reference will be taken from the title page of the publication.

5. In the bibliography, you use the details as they are given in the book or journal article.

5a. Reference to a book: Author's surname, initials, Year of publication. *Title*. Edition (if not the first). Place of publication: Publisher.

5b. Reference to a contribution in a book: Contributing author's surname, initials, Year of publication. 'Title of contribution'. Followed by Initials and surname of author or editor of publication followed by ed. or eds if relevant, *Title of book*. Place of publication: Publisher, page number(s) of contribution.

5c. Reference to an article in a journal: Author's surname, initials, Year of publication. 'Title of article', *Title of journal*,

Volume number and (part number), page numbers of contribution.

5d. Reference to a conference paper: Contributing author's surname, initials, Year of publication. 'Title of contribution'. Followed by: Title of conference proceedings, including date and place of conference.

5e. Reference to a thesis: Author's surname, initials, Year of publication. 'Title of thesis'. Designation (any type). Name of institution to which submitted.

Electronic material

1. Make sure readers can see exactly which information is being cited or quoted from an electronic source.

2. Always refer to a specific document and not simply home pages or menu pages.

3. Make sure the internet address is one which works!

4. A reference to an internet source must provide a title or description, a date (either the date of publication or update or the date of retrieval) and an address (uniform resource locator, or URL). Where you can, identify the authors of a document as well.

5. The most important element is the URL. Make sure the URL does not fail when accessed. Thus, give the exact address and double-check for updates if these are relevant.

Example
Felluga, Dino. 'Modules on Lacan: On the Structure of the Psyche.' *Introductory Guide to Critical Theory*. Date of last update, which you can find on the home page Purdue University. Date you accessed the site. <http://www.purdue. edu/guidetotheory/psychoanalysis/lacanstructure.html>

14 COMMON ERRORS IN WRITING AND PRESENTING

In academic writing, seminars and presentations, a number of common errors are repeatedly made by students in the first year of university. Errors are to be expected when working to deadlines, especially when other work is due at the same time, or when ideas are complex and it is difficult to translate them into the language of an essay. Listed below in italics are some of the most common ones with brief comments as to how to overcome the error.

OVER-GENERALISATIONS, GENERALISATIONS AND SWEEPING STATEMENTS

There is little doubt that film noir has served as a model for all good films since the 1950s. It is a genre which is beyond compare – inside and outside the film industry.

I agree with the critic and would join him in arguing that all popular television drama is unsophisticated.

And it is this cultural theory which is most suitable in the analysis of popular texts. No other theory comes close and this is supported in all the textbooks I consulted for the essay.

The main point to note about sweeping statements and generalisations is that, while they might be fine in conversations, they don't really stand up to closer scrutiny or analysis. They are invariably unsubstantiated, and they are the kinds of statements which essay markers call into doubt straightaway.

SUBJECTIVIST AND OVER-PERSONAL – A STEP UP FROM THE SWEEPING STATEMENT

I personally feel that the films of Alfred Hitchcock have never been surpassed, either for tone or style, since his death.

I truly believe Stephen Spielberg is the best director ever, and this recent film is yet another example of his utter mastery of film art because it is brilliantly made and has an excellent script.

In my considered view, there is no doubt that television has contributed to increased social disorder and moral laxity.

Comments of a deeply personal nature have their place, but need to be considered very carefully before being included in an academic essay. Like sweeping generalisations, they are difficult to justify in academic discourse and would probably be commented upon by the marker.

PROBLEMS WITH PHRASING . . .

I can follow that point of view, but your point of view is not the same as the one expressed by the others' points of view.

. . . AND STRUCTURE

Having said that, sci-fi is the best genre ever, and not agreeing with critics that of course it has its limitations, there is some sense that we can disagree that it is still the best genre.

Phrasing and sentence structure should add to the flow and readability of the essay. The above examples make the essay difficult to follow. Some 'advanced' academic writing is often guilty of endless qualification of points in one (very long) sentence, though poor phrasing and complex phrasing are not to be confused. Be as clear as possible.

SPELLING MISTAKES AND 'SILLY' ERRORS

The Wizard of Oz (1999) was directed by Ian Fleming and starred Judy Garlend.

His family wanted him to do all he could've.

The camcorder is shown with up-beat music and as the hip-hop music amplifies the feel.

It should be Victor Fleming; Ian wrote the Bond novels; the year is 1939; and the name is Gar<u>land</u>. These errors are usually avoided in essays which have been read and reread in draft form and read for the final time the day before submitting for formal assessment.

IRRELEVANT INFORMATION

The sequence is a very long sequence and some parts dwell and dwell over the hill but all in all, all the sequences are good and long.

This is my favourite television series ever and I have seen it twenty times in order to analyse it as best I can for this dissertation.

Again, irrelevant information is partly because the essay hasn't been checked before it was handed in, and partly because research and reading mean that it is padded out – something to be avoided in exams.

AMBIGUITY

I can see the man with the telescope.

Who has the telescope?

The food tastes of ancient people.

Does the sentence mean 'the food is awful' or 'the eating habits of ancient civilisations'?

I can fish.

There are at least three readings of the clause: 'can' meaning s/he is able to; 'can' meaning the person has a permit to fish; and 'can' as in the verb 'to can' fish. Ambiguity is an interesting feature in writing. On the one hand, ambiguity can mean that objects, terms or phrases are ambiguous because they are open to more than one meaning (a favourite discussion in the field of semiotics and post-structuralism!). On the other hand, ambiguity in academic writing can mean that the writing has been rushed. The above examples are obvious enough, but rushing an essay often means that the arguments are not as clear as they should or could be.

BIBLIOGRAPHY

A separate section discusses the Harvard System and bibliography, but take care before including any of the following as references:

Lecture Notes: universities discourage students from using lecture notes as major or minor source in essays. Apart from the fact that the essay should demonstrate extensive reading and research, you may have misheard what was being said and present an incorrect argument. Lecture notes are fine when being used for examination revision but most lectures and module guides provide readings lists of books and journal articles.

Internet sites: Using lots of internet sites (unless for the specific purpose of discussing particular web pages) suggests that the writer didn't need to use any books. Internet sites should only be used in moderation.

When quoting from a source, always be exact: provide author details, page number and date of publication. Make sure that the source in the body of the essay is backed up in the bibliography by a book or article with author or source details. The bibliography is important because it allows the reader to gain a sense of your research and data collection. The main sources will be mostly academic books and journal articles, though the latter may only become important during the second and third years of study.

Plagiarism: All universities have policies regarding plagiarism (passing someone's work off as your own and without any honest and judicious acknowledgement of sources). A bibliography, alongside specific page numbers for quotes in the body of the essay, allows the reader to see that you have incorporated sources and references.

15   EXAMINATIONS

In this chapter, some typical examination questions, from a cross-section of media and cultural studies degree programmes, are considered. The questions allow you to have an idea of the topics that will be assessed, as well as the ways in which the questions are asked. It is more than likely that the questions are phrased and structured along similar lines to A levels or Highers, although the content and themes are more typical of the undergraduate study of media and culture.

PHRASING OF QUESTIONS

One of the first points to make about examinations is that the marker – a member of staff who has taught on the degree or who is familiar with the range of ideas – is not looking for or expecting the student to recite everything that can be said about a topic. It is more a case of responding in ways which demonstrate your command of the key debates, and your confidence in discussing these issues with some fluency and critical sense. Questions require students to respond in certain ways and not others. Understanding these question 'stems' is important, and so the most common ones used in examinations are listed here.

Examine. This word is asking students to provide a relatively thorough written investigation of a particular debate, topic or object. 'To examine' means to look closely at something from a number of angles. You will ask probing questions and provide answers so that the shape and potential flaws of the object under examination become familiar. But you will also point to the strengths, as you see them, on the basis of your specific examination.

Discuss. Here you are being asked to approach a question in different ways. There is no one correct way to discuss a topic. However, it is often worth considering the ways in which your discussion focuses on one or two issues more than others in order to illustrate in detail what it is that is being discussed. See the word 'discuss' as a way of engaging the issues in diverse and stimulating ways. Consider, for instance, how discussions occur on television documentaries or on radio interviews. The best discussions come from participants who cover the range of material in interesting and sometimes provocative ways, but who do not stray from the subject.

How far has . . . This kind of phrase is making it clear to students that there is a number of ways of thinking about a particular topic. The answer will probably address the length and breadth of an issue or field. Again, it will be worth having one or two areas for specific illustration to support the answer.

Compare and contrast. This sort of question uses words which make clear that there are least TWO sides to a debate. Generally, to compare one thing with another is to see similarity, and to contrast one thing with another is to notice difference. The answer thus needs to indicate similarity and difference. Try and provide unusual contrasts in order to make the answer richer or more thought provoking.

Define and outline. These words are often used in conjunction with other key terms (as in 'Outline and examine . . .'). To outline and define a topic is to offer a fairly short summary without going into critical detail. Having defined 'culture', for instance, you will be expected to assess its usefulness or examine its different meanings.

Describe. To describe an object is not to express any judgement or make any assessment of its worth. You will be asked, for instance, to describe some of the features of contemporary youth cultures or the features of a particular television genre, and then go on to analyse, discuss or examine the features.

Assess and *evaluate*. These words are associated with the exercise of judgement, and often have an element of *measurement* attached to them, depending on the phrasing of the question.

Other terms such as *briefly*, *choose* and *drawing on the work of* are fairly self-explanatory but should always be taken into account in the interpretation of the examination question. In addition, always double check 'either/or' questions so that you are not answering both parts of the question if this is not required. Sometimes questions use quotations from other texts to elicit student responses. On some occasions, it will be necessary to know the work of the author, whereas, on other occasions, the quote is being used to stimulate discussion of a particular area of study.

EXAMPLES OF QUESTIONS

Module: Introduction to Cultural Studies and Popular Culture
Instructions: Answer TWO questions.
Time: 9.30 a.m. to 11.00 a.m.

1. Examine the role of popular fiction in relation to ONE of the following: gender identities; masculinity; childhood.
2. Discuss the links that can made between popular music and subcultural protest.
3. Some consider *Americanisation* a negative thing, some consider it positive, and some believe *Americanisation* hasn't happened. State briefly what is meant by this term, presenting an argument which indicates what your own position is in relation to any aspect of 'American culture' in the context of a country other than the USA.
4. Discuss the different ways in which audiences can 'read' television programmes, paying attention EITHER to the way the programme has been put together OR in relation to the notion of 'audience'.
5. 'The Frankfurt School offers limited insight into how popular culture can be understood'. How do you assess the influence

of their position in relation to current understandings of popular culture?

6. Choosing any popular text (film, music lyrics, novel, other) discuss how your chosen text represents life in cities.

7. How has your study of a specific cultural theory deepened your understanding of popular culture.

Module: Level I: Themes and Issues
Instructions: Answer TWO questions.
Time: 9.30 a.m. to 11.00 a.m.

1. Compare and contrast the work of Matthew Arnold and F. R. Leavis with Richard Hoggart's approach to the study of culture in his *The Uses of Literacy*.

2. Discuss Raymond Williams's contribution to the definition and study of ONE of the following: society; culture; communications; tradition.

3. With reference to specific examples, examine how a Marxist perspective can be used EITHER in the study of culture OR mass media.

4. Briefly outline the meaning of 'subculture' and analyse how subcultures challenge dominant cultural practices.

5. Examine how a theory of the sign has been used EITHER in the study of culture OR the study of mass media.

6. 'I resented seeing Nature and History confused at every turn, and I wanted to track down, in the decorative display of *what-goes-without-saying*, the ideological abuse which is hidden there' (Roland Barthes: *Mythologies*, 1957). Examine Barthes's claim, discussing specific examples to support your explanation.

Media Studies
Instructions: Answer TWO questions.
Time: 9.30 a.m. to 11.00 a.m.

1. On the basis of your studies in this module, outline and assess the contribution of EITHER audience research OR theories and methods of content analysis to the study of contemporary media.

2. Drawing on specific examples, discuss the relations between the media and globalisation and/or imperialism.

3. 'Television news is never impartial'. Explore this claim, providing specific examples in your answer.
4. Examine the media's role in the production and consumption of celebrities.
5. 'There is no such thing as "Reality-TV".' Discuss this claim in relation to specific output.
6. Discuss the media's role in the construction of ONE of the following: time; events; space; locality; sociality.
7. Examine the role of the radio in the representation and/or construction of 'community'.
8. What, in your view, is the most important matter which confronts media organisations today?

Media and Communications
Instructions: Answer Question 1 and any other question.
Time: 9.30 a.m. to 11.00 a.m.

1. The News. Choose any THREE topics and offer a critical summary in relation to how media studies understands the news. You are encouraged to make references to research and empirical evidence. Each summary should be approximately one page long.
   a/ news agencies; b/ news frameworks; c/ agenda setting; d/ news globalisation; e/ CNN; f/ the filter model; g/ news values; h/ propaganda; i/ ITN.
   This is a compulsory question.
2. Discuss whether audiences are more usefully understood as citizens or as consumers.
3. How far are media professionals constrained by media organisations?
4. Compare and contrast discourse analysis with EITHER frame analysis OR semiotics.
5. Discuss the ways in which a sociological analysis of the media differs from a cultural studies analysis.
6. Critically explore the conflicting interpretations of globalisation.
7. Outline what is meant by 'media discourse' and examine how the media uses discourses of EITHER ethnicity OR social class.

BEFORE AND DURING EXAMINATIONS

Most students have studied for examinations before going to university. Examinations aim to assess undergraduates' abilities to recall and discuss knowledge in a set time period – usually forty-five minutes per question. It is not necessary to know every single detail or fact. However, it is important to demonstrate a command of the field and an ability to focus on detail by providing useful illustrations of knowledge. Reproducing everything you think will be required to answer the question is not usually what is required by examiners. Rather, demonstrating an ability to discuss in reflective and critical ways is a much better indication of students' knowledge and skills.

Before

Preparation and planning: In many ways, this starts when the module does, and so always keep detailed notes which can be broken down into key points and used constructively in future revision.

Revision: Always start earlier than you think you should, and revise in short but productive time periods.

Planning: Identify the days when you will revise, the topics you will revise, and stick to the plans.

Note-making: Make notes and know the ideas to which the notes refer. Reading and note-making go hand-in-hand. Sometimes diagrams and summary lists are useful ways of remembering what it is you need to recall in the examination. Highlight key names and concepts.

Previous papers: It can be useful to look at previous examination questions.

Underpinning Logic: Always have in mind a rationale or an approach which will structure your answer. Foreground critical approaches when revising, and be clear about it in the note-making and general preparation. Use evidence and remember key names if relevant, drawing attention to the relevance of themes, theories and perspectives which the module has covered.

During

Structure: In the examination, briefly map out the structure of your response to the question, consider how the question is asking you to respond, and make reference to the question at least three or four times in the answer. If a key point should have been included, make a note of where it should have been, using an asterisk or arrow.

Timing: If the exam questions are equally weighted, make sure the same amount of time is spent on each question. Answer your preferred or your 'second-best' question first as this can build up confidence and allow more time for questions you are less certain about.

Signposting: State the obvious in examination answers and provide signposts of what you know and how the essay will develop.

Style: Do not worry too much about exactness of style and phrasing; the examination essay usually reads better than you think. However, do write legibly.

Repetition: Do not repeat material in the same answers or in other essays.

Anxiety: Remember that anxiety is normal in examination conditions, and remind yourself that you have passed examinations before!

The module and examinations

Remember that all modules:

1. have key themes and concepts. Remind yourself of these before and during the examination.

2. are associated with names of theorists and theories. Again, remind yourself of these before and during the examination.

3. have a rationale and aims and objectives which underpin the module. Make sure you are aware of this rationale while revising.

Make sure that examination answers or coursework essays deal with these features. It is often useful to make reference to what the module has covered and how this has impacted on your studies.

Some examinations are essay based; some are short-answer based; some examinations use multiple choice questions; and some are text based or provide stimulus material to comment on. Make sure you know how you are being assessed. However, also remember that, in many ways, the key skills in essay-based examination are those associated with essay writing. Developing skills in essay writing are the ones which will stand you in good stead in examinations.

Stimulus material

Some examinations will provide an extract to be read in timed conditions. You will normally be asked to comment on the extract by way of short answers. Examinations which provide stimulus material for comment are assessing skills of reading, knowledge, comprehension, interpretation, summary, précis and discussion. An extract below gives you some idea of how to respond to these types of assessments. Typically, stimulus material is followed by questions, whose weighting is indicated in brackets, and which gives you some sense of the amount of time to spend on each response.

Examination: Myths in media and culture
Instructions:

1. Read the stimulus material below.
2. Answer ALL questions.

Time: 9.00 a.m. to 10.15 a.m.

The relations between production, output, consumption, and identity have been central to the research and analysis of the media and culture industries over the last twenty years. The recent Open University course D318 'Culture, Media and Identities' has as two of its key textbooks <u>Representation</u>: *Cultural Representations and Signifying Practices* (1997; ed. Stuart Hall), and *Doing Cultural Studies: The Story of the Sony Walkman* (1997; eds du Gay et al.). Both volumes present research findings structured around and informed by the 'circuit of culture', a model which allows culture to be analysed in terms of representation, identity, production, consumption and regulation (Hall, ed., 1997: 1–11). Fundamental to the concepts of media and culture in the Open University course and textbook series is language, <u>and the key feature of language is its function as a 'representational system'</u>. Indeed, at the centre and at the edges of the circuit of culture is the domain of representation. Representations – both in the OU series and more generally in some recent culture study are understood in relation of the notion of 'texts'. <u>Roland Barthes's discussion of the myths which structure contemporary mass culture proposes that textual representations are neither natural nor neutral</u>. His *Mythologies* (1957) demonstrates how signs and texts are caught up in a history whose apparent inevitability is attributable not to an uncontrollable nature but to the force fields of myth and ideology.

<u>In Barthes's work, human subjects are also texts and are textual, cultural more than they are simply 'natural'</u>. *Mythologies* is concerned to expose how culture masquerades as nature via the imperatives of the myth. But Barthes's is an exposition which has the additional effect of highlighting the significance of the cultural consumption of myths. Faces, magazines, sporting events, striptease shows and eating and drinking are examples which Barthes uses in his attempt to show how myths are made meaningful in relation to

their cultural consumption, social exchange and symbolic usage. His essay 'The face of Greta Garbo' (*Mythologies* 56–7) succinctly attends to the ways in which subjects' faces and physiologies become embodied not on the basis of impartiality or biology but in the situations of the signs and practices of socio-cultural histories. Garbo's cinematic face plunged audiences into 'the deepest ecstasy' (56). The impact of the star is not simply linked to her filmic or celebrity status but to the subsequent conceptual consumption of the Garbo in the cinematic and cultural economy. In Barthes's account, it is clear that consumption is tied to notions of identity and language: 'As a language, Garbo's singularity was of the order of the concept, that of Audrey Hepburn is of the order of the substance. The face of Garbo is an Idea, that of Hepburn, an Event' (57).

Questions

1. What does the opening paragraph identify as the key issues in recent media and cultural analysis? (20%)
2. How are these issues linked to the research of Roland Barthes? (20%)
3. What, in your view, is meant by 'myth' in the extract above? (20%)
4. Making links with your studies in this module, comment critically any TWO of the sections underlined in the above extract. (40%)

16   SEMINARS AND GROUP WORK

1. Seminars are smaller than lectures and are ideally composed of no more than fifteen students and a lecturer.

2. The seminar is the space where ideas and issues are disseminated, discussed, debated and explored. They are an essential part of university learning (and assessment in some cases), and are as important as lectures, tutorials, workshops and production meetings.

3. There is no one way to do a seminar, but they are usually structured in very informal ways, with the group ideally seated facing each other. Sometimes the seminar will be organised around one key topic. On other occasions, it may be that stimulus material (for example, a handout or article, with supporting questions) has been provided, and students prepare for the seminar the week before the group meets.

4. Ideally, every student makes some form of contribution, either in a smaller group of two or three in the seminar itself, or as part of the general group discussion. Seminars are to be welcomed with enthusiasm, and they are potentially very enjoyable elements in the learning and teaching process. Undoubtedly students often feel nervous about sharing ideas in this kind of setting, but there's no reason that seminars shouldn't be one of the best places to learn.

ENJOYING SEMINARS

1. Students should not feel intimated. Media and culture studies are principally concerned with how people live

with each other in relation to the objects, forms, institutions and practices of the media. Culture is a way of life which is not fixed but open for debate and discussion – and so use the seminar to engage with some passion and humour.

2. Seminars are the place to state what it is about the lecture or the module that is straightforward, complex, interesting, obvious, worth talking about further or not worth talking about again.

3. The seminar is the place to make your own mark on how media, culture and society are talked about.

4. The seminar is not for the lecturers! At least, lecturers give lectures and students do seminars. The lecturer's role in the seminar is to facilitate the discussion.

5. Don't think lecturers are expecting right answers and that wrong answers will be mocked. Think of the seminar as something which is undertaken in a spirit of inquiry and open discussion.

SEMINAR ACTIVITIES: CULTURE, CONSUMPTION AND EVERYDAY LIFE

Below is an example of a cultural studies seminar on 'reading'. This is material provided at the beginning of the seminar (which lasts an hour). The seminar brief accompanied the lecture of the previous day (which was on the theme of consumer cultures). The example is included here in order to provide students with a sense of how seminars are not to be feared. It is a forum in which to challenge, question and understand different positions and arguments. In addition, seminars are great places for understanding the ideas that will be used in the writing of the essay for a module, etc.

Key aim: to explore the relationships between identity and the production and consumption of 'texts'.

Task One: What is *identity*? What defines or describes your own identity? Is identity the same as (a) personality (b) individual (c) subject

Task Two: READING (novels, comics, magazines, internet site, other)

- How do you define 'reading'?
- How does reading define you?
- Is reading a production- or consumption-based activity?
- A novel: is the author the most important figure in the determination of meaning.
- What is meant by 'the death of the author' and 'the birth of the reader'?
- 'Meaning IS fixed in the text.' Discuss.
- 'Meaning is NOT fixed in the text.' Discuss.
- What's the relationship between consuming a text and producing an identity?
- What reading skills are required in a media-literate society?

GROUP WORK

Some assignments at degree level are assessed wholly or in part by means of group-work projects and presentations. Sometimes the group is required to respond to a particular theoretical brief (along the lines of the seminar activity above), a piece of ethnographic or audience research, or team task in a production-based group (see 'Production projects', p. 000).

Group work means you will need to:

1. Consider the extent to which a common or collective understanding of the task has been thought through.

2. Ensure that each group member is in agreement with decisions or strategies.

3. Agree tasks and share roles and responsibilities.

4. Make sure that all group members understand how work will be assessed, and how far the task is assessed on individual contributions.

5. Book equipment, rooms, fix meeting times.

6. Establish group-working practices.

7. Agree deadlines, time limits and timescales.

8. Be prepared to confront conflict directly, and agree any changes to plans collectively.

9. Agree to monitor workloads and outputs.

17 DISSERTATIONS, RESEARCH PROJECTS AND PRODUCTIONS

EXTENDED RESEARCH PROJECTS

A research project or dissertation demonstrate a student's continued input and research effort over a prolonged period, and they are key ways of assessing work in the final year of study. The research project itself will very much depend on the sort of degree programme being followed. It is possible to identify three routes, depending on the degree route being pursued:

Dissertation

This will be a piece of written work, not usually less than 8,000 words, which investigates a key question and is presented in the form of a detailed argument. The analysis and discussion will be structured according to specific conventions, but normally include the abstract, introduction, specific chapters, conclusion and record of sources used. The dissertation is a fairly standard option on media studies, film studies and cultural studies programmes. Examples later in the chapter illustrate some of the ways of doing dissertations and production projects.

Employment-related project OR audience research project

This is a piece of work which draws on and/or combines strategies such as ethnography, social research, quantitative analysis and organisational theory with the aim of providing useful data on the basis of a specific research question. This route usually involves working with a local group or community, a business or media organisation, using questionnaires, survey methods or ethnographic methods. This kind of research is fairly typical of degree programmes which combine media and/or cultural studies or media production with journalism, marketing, business studies, sociology, psychology or other social science courses.

Production project

This route is one that is often taken by students on production-based degree courses. The project will usually entail the production of a final piece of work (for example, short film, radio broadcast, newspaper articles, photographic exhibition). This is an ideal way for production students to demonstrate skills in, for example, sound, editing, reporting, medium-specific skills, working with others in crew and putting together a production which is assessed by staff and increasingly by peers. The project is usually supported by an accompanying rationale which justifies and discusses the logic of the project.

Common features
Before offering some examples of initial proposals and final research project proposals, it is possible to identify some of the common features of the three different research projects, and the reasons why projects such as these are used in final assessments.

1. They provide an opportunity to engage in extended research over a prolonged period.

2. A key idea or proposal can be developed thoroughly.

3. A range of skills can be assessed at the same time.

4. Final-year projects mean students can develop specialisms.

5. The project is something which can be usefully and profitably discussed on CVs and job applications.

6. The project assesses the linkages between critical, intellectual, analytic, generic, practical and employability skills.

7. Projects can often lead to postgraduate study or specific employment routes.

Research, whether in the form of a dissertation, an extended essay or social-scientific investigation or ethnographic project, will be presented in accordance with the practices and conventions of the university. However, a number of observations may be made which will assist students new to this kind of assessment. The final piece of work will always have:

1. A front cover which is also a title page.

2. An abstract (of no more than one side of A4) which offers in summary form an overview of the project.

3. A contents page (list of section, chapters, sub-sections, etc.).

4. A list of sources and/or bibliography.

5. Appendices (optional).

One of the most common ways of bringing together the information or the content is as follows:

1. Introduction; or statement of aims and objectives.

2. Review of sources, or literature review

3. Methods; or methodology

4. Discussion of results.

5. Conclusion

Variations might include:

1. Introduction.

2. Chapters or sections.

3. Conclusion.

Details of structures

The abstract: an abstract states in summary form the context of a research project. It outlines briefly the background, purpose and context of the project and provides a résumé of the research methods used, the findings and the conclusion. It does not offer detailed discussion, and it does not comment in critical or evaluative ways. The abstract is not normally longer than one side of A4, word-processed and single spaced.

The introduction: the introduction should describe the context and the setting of the research project, allowing the reader to gain a sense of its purpose, aims and objectives, and why these matter in relation to the chosen field. The introduction will explain the reasons for the way that the research has been carried out in the way it has, and may identify some of the very specific questions that have been considered.

Literature/sources review: this is a section which might be included in the introduction or across introductory chapters of the dissertation. However, the main aim of the literature review is to establish that your research shows: (1) links with key research in the field; (2) your knowledge of which research (journals, books, other) is the most recent and the most relevant; and (3) that you are alert to and address key concepts, perspectives and theories. The review can be organised in a number of ways, but generally short extracts or citations from key texts are grouped around themes or chronology or approaches. If the dissertation is concerned with popular culture, then it might be that the literature review breaks down the broad area into more manageable segments (for example, popular youth cultures, theories of popular culture, popular music, youth cultures, and popular youth cultures and girls). Literature reviews arranged chronologically will discuss material by date of publication. Thus, a dissertation on audience studies and media reception will deal with material from the 1950s, 1960s, 1970s and so on. Or, it may deal with material in terms of key responses to a piece of work over a twenty-year period (for example, responses to Hall's encoding/

decoding model from 1973 to 1993). A literature review which is organised around themes may well select material which draws on feminist, Marxist and semiotic approaches to media audiences.

Methodology: this section is more relevant to some dissertations than others. In the case of the dissertation proposal, it may be that the section on methodology is not a major part of the dissertation or research project. Let's imagine the dissertation is an investigation into how audiences interpret the national TV news in a one-week period. The section on methodology will provide an overview of the research questions which the dissertation is examining. It will then consider specifically 'who' the audience or the sample is and whether the interview sample should be organised according to age, location, social class, gender, family group or other criteria. In your methodology, you should be attentive to the methods of sampling, the restrictions which might impair the work undertaken, and the procedures that will be adopted for data collection. It may be that the dissertation needs to demonstrate analyses in statistical ways, making links between quantitative and qualitative data. All data collection and interpretation needs to be accurate, but accuracy can be understood in different ways.

Results and discussions: there is no one correct way to present results or discussions of data. Often the university will provide students with guidelines appropriate to the degree programme being studied. Some dissertations will present results separately followed by discussion of them. If a results section is required:

1. Present your findings in charts, tables, or figure so that general trends or problems can be seen at a glance.

2. List important findings, results, patterns, exceptions and trends.

3. Comment on the results, especially where the most important findings are concerned.

4. Present these findings in logical and sequential ways (for example, 1, 1.1, 1.1a, etc.). Again, the conventions of how to do this will be listed in the university's guidelines.

Discussion of results can vary, although all discussions should make reference to the main aims and objectives of the research project. The most important findings and questions should be discussed in thorough ways, and should draw on a literature review and your own critical analysis and appraisal. The discussions will allow you to consider a range of explanations, hypotheses, etc.

Conclusion: in an extended piece of work, the conclusion should consider a range of implications and amplify the arguments made throughout the project. You might consider making recommendations, suggesting strategies for future work or investigation, note areas for improvement or further development. No piece of work covers everything, and so there is no requirement to imply or claim that the research has exhausted all the issues.

PRODUCTION-BASED PROJECTS

In many media and cultural studies courses, there are opportunities to do an extended piece of work or project which relates to production modules. Production-based work can include journalism and writing for the media, photography, film, radio, digital media, web design or other media practice. The project might also be combined with work experience or an industrial placement. Many media-production-based programmes will require students to demonstrate technical skills and abilities in the use of media equipment, working according to professional codes and regulations, and in teams where decisions reflect individual initiative as well as group efforts. It is vital to check how the project will be assessed and to make sure that you identify the criteria you need to address.

It is worth briefly considering some of the specific topics within production modules which students might develop into research projects:

- screenwriting in the style of a particular programme genre
- production projects in the style of documentary genres or hybrid genres
- writing for a specific magazine and with a particular brief
- improving interpersonal communications in organisations
- radio news coverage of war and conflict
- media globalisation and cybercultures
- web design
- sound and audio studies
- media ethics and the reporting of conflict
- media ethics and photography
- interactive DVD
- radio drama

Examples of projects

It is usually the case that you will study 'research' modules during the second year of the course which prepare you for the research and study skills required at level III. However, students usually find that there are one or two key topics which interest them and which will be developed into research or production projects at level III.

If we take the radio news module from the list above, how might a proposal develop from the taught classes? A group of students might decide to conduct research in the local community or on behalf of a specific group with the aim of producing a radio broadcast. (Organisations might commission the group to do the research.) The topic which interested the group in the radio module was 'radio news and representing disability and social marginality'. One way of imagining the project is as follows:

1. A number of residents who use Age Concern are increasingly alarmed by the decline in public transport links between the city centre and the suburbs.

2. You (and your group) are a radio production/broadcast team based at the local station, and you have agreed as a team to investigate the matter.

3. The radio station has generously agreed a ten-minute slot on the sixty-minutes lunchtime news report.

(Further ways of imagining this production project include a double-page report in the local newspaper produced by one student, a series of articles over a four-week period produced by a team of students or a report for a TV station, also produced by a team of students.)

For the purposes of the team assessment, the project might involve:

1. a group of students who will agree specific tasks and roles for which they are individually assessed;

2. students keeping a portfolio of evidence which documents their contributions and reflections; and

3. students assessing other members' ongoing contributions in the production of the radio bulletin.

Responsibility for the project is divided among the group of students (group as well as individual pieces are assessed).

1. The end product (for example, radio report or short film in the case of visual texts) will be broadcast or screened to tutors and peers. Specific criteria will be used to assess the quality of the piece. Each member of the group will receive

an individual mark (based on agreed contributions and roles) and a group mark. The portfolio of evidence will also contribute to the individual mark of each group member.

2. A group report (or an executive summary) of the project's rationale will discuss the extent to which the group achieved what it set out to do. Often this takes the form of the final report which accompanies the production itself. Remember: it is the production proposal or rationale which makes the project seem viable or not, and so it is important to map out your production rationale clearly and convincingly (see below).

Two other examples of production projects might include interactive DVD and television documentary production. Interactive DVD projects will allow students to show advanced skills in new media production, demonstrating in addition a critical knowledge of recent technology, and competent production management skills. Production files will allow the student to show abilities and critical skills in being able to evaluate and contextualise their production work in relation to theoretical and practical concerns. Similarly, a practical project in TV documentary production will allow students to combine theoretical and practical skills in a project which results in a video documentary. It is more than likely that this project will be group based. Students will be assessed on their knowledge of production techniques but also in relation to detailed fieldwork and research, allowing the group to evidence a knowledge and understanding of the processes of the media industry. The rationale of the project will also be assessed by means of pre-production and production files, and subsequent production management. As with all practical projects, it is important to allow the final production piece to express your knowledge of underpinning concepts and knowledge of media and cultural theories. A critical awareness of intended audience, the reception contexts, the politics of representation and the economic and industrial contexts would be considered and reflected in the rationale, the draft scripts and the management of the piece.

PRODUCTION RATIONALE

The projects listed above all assume a production rationale or justification. Some of the questions which would be addressed at the outset of the project are listed below.

Rationale – why do you intend to carry out this production?

- Why are you interested in this production project?
- What is the key idea or ideas which informs the production project?
- What will the production finally demonstrate?
- How does it relate to other productions in the field?

Approaches to production

- What materials will the production use or require?
- Who is involved in the production and why?
- If the production involves external agencies, how will you access your target groups?
- What information will you get from them and how will you record it?
- Why do you think your production is best tackled the way you propose?

Organising and planning

- What do you think your biggest problems will be (scale, materials, personnel, etc.), and how do you propose to resolve them?
- How will the actual production take shape?
- How will it be organised over the period allocated for the production?

DOING PRODUCTION PROJECTS

In all production projects – whether based on individual or group assessment – it is vital that the production tutors can sense that:

1. The aims and objectives are clearly stated.
2. The structure of the project is explicit.
3. A clear outline of roles and responsibilities of individual students is obvious from the start.
4. The weighting of individual contributions is made clear from the outset (often this is set by the module or the degree course).

Make sure that tutors can gauge how the project will:

1. address the specific issues of the production brief;
2. allow abilities to be assessed in relation to production-specific skills as well as underlying theoretical knowledge; and
3. enable all group members to demonstrate individual and collective working practices.

18   MEDIA PRODUCTION COURSES

Chapter 1, 'What Are the Media? What Is Media Studies', out-lines in fairly general terms how media studies and media production degrees are structured. However, there are some students who, while they may have taken media studies at GCSE or 'A' level, have limited experience of media production before going to university. This section offers more detailed observations and comments, and aims to encourage students who don't have media skills or training not to be deterred from making inquiries about studying media production.

EXPERIENCES OF MEDIA PRODUCTION

No two media production courses are the same. Each will have slightly different aims and objectives. In large media studies departments, there will also be variations based on specialist interests (for example, new media, video production, print journalism). However, the main points to note about media production can be summarised as follows:

1. You will be trained in a range of media production skills (ranging from newspaper journalism to working in sound), and it is usual for students to attend classes in media theory and critical studies.

2. The production degree will train students to produce work for a variety of audiences and target groups. Journalism students, for instance, may well have to produce a newspaper or magazine, and have responsibilities which cover a range of skills.

3. The professional skills acquired in media production degrees will invariably relate closely to experiences in the media industries and media organisations. The skills acquired will be media based and related closely to professional and industrial practice. In addition, interpersonal, administrative and intellectual abilities will be developed.

4. Working in the media industries also means working to tight deadlines and under constraints determined by audiences as well as the media organisation. Thus, time-management skills will be emphasised throughout your development on the media degree.

5. Media programme makers, in addition to learning how to meet external deadlines, will also make programmes for external agencies, and the degree course will provide opportunities and experiences to demonstrate skills in these areas.

6. Often, degree programmes will facilitate work placements or allow students to consolidate employability skills. Experiences might include: working in design companies; shadowing key personnel in marketing, advertising and PR companies; doing a job (or shadowing) in local newsrooms (for example, in television or in the press office); working with the voluntary sector on the production of promotional or campaign-based materials; and working in university PR and marketing departments. Most degree programmes also encourage students to seek out media placements of their own choosing, in the UK or abroad.

Examples of modules

The 'skills' side of a media production degree is important, but the skills themselves are always integrally connected to the wider theoretical and conceptual questions of broadcasting, culture and society, and the media. We can consider these links in relation to a number of fairly typical production modules that may be taught at level I.

Journalism

An introductory module in journalism, for instance, will develop students' knowledge of some of the key terms and concepts of the newspaper industry. Skills will usually be taught in small classes which deal with understanding how the newspaper industry operates. Although students will learn how to write according to different newspaper formats and genres, critical study of the format or genre will be as important as the actual skills acquired. Journalism requires knowledge of social and political issues, and it also requires knowledge of ethics in the context of the media. Skills in interviewing and researching, newsgathering and copy presentation will be taught in relation to theories concerning the role of the journalist and the function of news reporting in contemporary societies.

Television studio

Similarly, a module such as 'The Television Studio' will also be skills based, and will be organised around planning, structuring and recording 'as live' a news programme. Work in television studios, however, also requires solid grounding in the operation of a television studio, multi-camera work and other equipment as well as knowledge and experience of production roles. However, these skills will be acquired in a context which asks questions about television and public service broadcasting, digital media, and deregulation. Alongside learning a range of procedures and techniques (for example, training in vision mixing, floor managing, directing and camera operating), students will appraise their work in relation to others, or present a file of the student's own critical assessment of television viewing.

Cybercultures

Increasingly, students on media studies and media production degrees take modules in internet or web studies (an area which is often referred to as 'cybercultures'). Modules in this field provide excellent opportunities for linking theory, practice, critique and skills. A module in cybercultures will involve practical skills, but it will also establish a knowledge base for the understanding of the theoretical and conceptual issues surrounding identity, politics and globalisation. This is because the internet is as much about design, layout and technology as it is about theories of communication, the construction of virtual communities and concepts of space. A module in cybercultures, then, might examine the history of the internet and the emergence of cyber-communities, encouraging students to examine issues which encompass online fan cultures, the politics of digital copyright and language and identification in the new media. This is also an area which proves very rich for dissertation research.

Radio production

A radio production module, for instance, will introduce students to the methods and techniques of radio production. Sessions might consider studio operations and functions, knowledge and production of live radio sequences, and investigation of radio formats and genres. But because radio is in very obvious, and perhaps not-so-obvious ways, a medium of voice and speech, so students will be trained to assess and critique the language and contexts of speech inside and outside radio. In addition, students might well produce a radio package according to a specific brief and conventions (see earlier chapters). In a radio module, intellectual and practical skills include researching, note-making, interviewing, digital editing, drafting/writing, studio operation and presentation. But because radio broadcasting is never detached from the society in which the medium makes sense, so a key part of the assessment in a radio module might involve listening to radio and compiling a radio log or portfolio.

Sound

Radio – but also television and film – are concerned with sound. Again, modules dealing with this area of media production prove interesting in terms of how sound is used to generate a sense of image, context and actuality. Modules concerned with sound recording will develop skills in using portable recorders and microphones, encouraging students to work with sound in a range of acoustic situations and conditions, and in order to generate different impacts. Moreover, creating and transferring digital audio files (MP3 and MIDI), or using a variety of sources for recording and subsequent editing, are abilities which will also be developed. However, to the extent that sound raises a number of important questions for the media (for example, the psychology of 'hearing' and 'listening'), so a module of this kind is as interesting in terms of its conceptual frameworks as much as its skills base.

MEDIA PRODUCTION: ASSESSMENTS

Each practical module will be assessed in slightly different ways. However, the following general guidelines provide a sense of how practical modules are marked.

1. It is important that the work is fully completed, especially where there are a number of elements being assessed. Never submit a project which is only half finished.

2. It is vital that the production or project demonstrates skills and competencies in the relevant medium. Moreover, if you are required to work to industry guidelines, make sure this is also brought out in the submitted piece.

3. All production modules require students to link theory and practice. Always demonstrate knowledge, where relevant, of cultural, social and ethical issues which the project or production might raise.

4. If management skills are being assessed, then these must be evidenced in portfolios, reports or summaries of work.

5. The critical evaluation of the project is essential. Make sure this covers in detail how you achieved what you set out to at the beginning of the project. Indicate where and why changes were made to original plans.

6. Make sure that the project shows your awareness of industrial and institutional concerns (where this is relevant).

19 EMPLOYABILITY AND PROGRESS FILES

The range of jobs media and cultural studies graduates enter is vast, and it includes media-based and non-media-based settings. Most universities train students to self-assess and monitor their 'employability skills'. This means that students are not simply receiving training in critical and practical skills but are additionally demonstrating skills in team work, communications and administration, leadership, and research.

CONTEXT AND HISTORY OF EMPLOYABILITY AND PROGRESS FILES

In the UK and elsewhere, degree programmes are monitored in various ways, and on a regular basis. Staff research output, publications and scholarly activities, alongside teaching quality are all assessed. Teaching quality is an important measure for staff and for students, and so is research. Assessment grades in these areas are available for all universities, though it has to be stressed that universities and degree programmes should be judged on a range of criteria and not simply 'official statistics'.

However, it is against this backdrop that students are increasingly asked to maintain progress files (PFs), and to monitor their employment skills. Briefly, progress files are records of the way a student has attempted to monitor their progress in intellectual, practical and personal ways whilst at university. 'Employability' refers to employment skills and the student's preparedness in:

1. working with others;
2. showing initiative and leadership;

enough; or students need regular reminders about the conventions of academic writing and are reluctant to ask for further guidance. Use the progress file system to log development issues such as these, and make small but important advances in progress. The progress file is a semi-structured and supportive process, and it should allow students to strengthen their relationship to their own learning, planning and reflection.

The progress file is a process associated with intellectual and critical activities which, ideally, should:

1. promote a greater insight into how you learn, how you study and how you research;

2. clarify how to increase independence and confidence in learning;

3. provide some sense of how to think and talk about employment and career possibilities after university;

4. provide some sense of direction in the field of postgraduate study and/or further training; and

5. promote positive approaches to study and learning

Portfolios of work

Modules which combine academic content with employability skills will often require students to submit portfolios of work. The portfolio will be used to assess your input on the module concerned, and it will demonstrate your ongoing investment and formation in a particular area of study. Often, research-based modules or modules which involve a number of components (for example, journalism) use portfolios as the principal means of assessment.

The following summary lists the elements which will comprise the portfolio of work.

Example
Module: Research and employment-related studies: Level II (20 credits)
All work will be submitted in a portfolio whose contents will be ordered as follows:
Progress File: This will cover the period of semester two. (15%)
Summary of findings: This will list the key findings of the ethnographic research (or other agreed research topic) undertaken within a small group. (500–700 words) (20%)
Annotated literature review: This will identity and summarise three key books or other academic sources used in research project/work. (1k words) (20%)
Job search: CV, job application form completed and 1,000 word summary of job search skills. (15%)
Personal Progress Presentation: This will be presented during the assessment sessions in week 9 or 10 of the module. (30%)

Assessment criteria
Portfolios of work will be assessed as follows:

1. Work submitted in the portfolio is detailed and clear.

2. Files, summaries, CVs and applications are presented in ways which make the aims and objectives of the module transparent.

3. Portfolios are ordered and structured.

4. Portfolios demonstrate evidence of self-critical reflection and application, and students' reflections show awareness of areas of strength and weakness in balanced and logical ways.

5. Action planning is clearly but realistically established, with aims and objectives built into progress files or self-reflections.

6. Students' critical reflections attempt to assess whether or not goals or the aims of research/learning aims have been achieved.

7. Where appropriate, projects have been undertaken and/or completed according to conventions and agreed formulae.

8. Students have attempted to synthesise prior experiences and learning, and have considered directions for further research or reading.

FURTHER READING IN STUDY SKILLS

Clark, V., Baker, J. and Lewis, E. (2002), *Key Concepts and Skills for Media Studies*, London: Hodder Arnold.

Cottrell, S. (2003), *The Study Skills Handbook*, Basingstoke: Palgrave, now Palgrave Macmillan.

Denscombe, M. (2002), *Ground Rules for Good Research: A 10 Point Guide for Social Researchers*, Buckingham: Open University Press.

Denscombe, M. (2003), *The Good Research Guide: For Small-scale Social Research Projects*, Buckingham: Open University Press.

Gaskell, P. (1998), *Standard Written English*, Edinburgh: Edinburgh University Press.

Hicks, W. and Adams, S. (2001), *Interviewing for Journalists*, London and New York: Routledge.

Keeble, R. (2001), *Ethics for Journalists*, London and New York: Routledge.

Peck, J. and Coyle, M. (1999), *The Student's Guide to Writing: Spelling, Punctuation and Grammar*, Basingstoke: Macmillan, now Palgrave Macmillan.

BIBLIOGRAPHY AND RECOMMENDED READING

The following books prove useful in the study of media and culture. They variously provide general outlines of the field, offer systematic coverage of key themes, concepts and theorists, stimulate further discussion, and supply details of further reading.

Barthes, R. (1973), *Mythologies*, London: Jonathan Cape.
Du Gay, P., Hall, S., Janes, L., Mackay, H. and Negus, K. (1997), *Doing Cultural Studies: The Story of the Sony Walkman*, London: Sage.
Hall, S. (ed.) (1997), *Representation: Cultural Representations and Signifying Practices*, London: Sage.
Hall, S., Hobson, D., Lowe, A. and Willis, P. (1992 (1980)), *Culture, Media, Language*, London: Routledge.
Marris, P. and Thornham, S. (1999), *Media Studies: A Reader*, Edinburgh: Edinburgh University Press.
Storey, J. (2001), *Cultural Theory and Popular Culture: An Introduction*, 3rd edn, Harlow: Pearson Education. http://cwx.prenhall.com/bookbind/pubbooks/storey_ema/. This also has exercises, self-assessments and a useful glossary of key terms.
Williams, R. (1965), *The Long Revolution*, Harmondsworth: Penguin.
Williams, R. (1988; 1976), *Keywords: A Vocabulary of Culture and Society*, London: Fontana.

BIBLIOGRAPHY AND SOURCES CONSULTED

Ang, I. (1985), *Watching Dallas*, London: Methuen.
Barthes, R. (1973), *Mythologies*, London: Jonathan Cape.
Bengston, D. N. and Fan, D. P. (1999), 'Conflict over Natural Resource Management: A Social Indicator on Analysis of Online News Media Text', *Society and Natural Resources*, 12: 493–500.
Berger, A. A. (1982), *Media Analysis Techniques*, London: Sage.
Burton, G. (2000), *Talking Television: An Introduction to the Study of Television*, London: Arnold.
Chomsky, N. (1991), *Deterring Democracy*, London and New York: Verso.

Chomsky, N. and Herman, E. S. (1988), *Manufacturing Consent: The Political Economy of the Mass Media*, New York: Pantheon.

Creeber, G. (ed.) (2001), *The Television Genre Book*, London: BFI.

Devereux, E. (2003), *Understanding the Media*, London: Sage.

Du Gay, P., Hall, S., Janes, L., Mackay, H. and Negus, K. (1997), *Doing Cultural Studies: The Story of the Sony Walkman*, London: Sage.

Entman, R. M. (1993), 'Framing: Towards clarification of a Fractured Paradigm', *Journal of Communication*, 43(4): 51–8.

Glasgow Media Group (1985), *War and Peace News*, London: Routledge and Kegan Paul.

Gripsrud, J. (2000), *Understanding Media Culture*, London: Hodder Arnold.

Hall, S. (ed.) (1997), *Representation: Cultural Representations and Signifying Practices*, London: Sage.

Hall, S., Hobson, D., Lowe, A. and Willis, P. (1992 (1980)), *Culture, Media, Language*, London: Routledge.

Hermes, J. (1995), *Reading Women's Magazines*, Cambridge: Polity.

Holland, P. (1997), *The Television Handbook*, London: Routledge.

Huston, A. C. (1992), *Big World, Small Screen: The Role of Television in American Society*, Lincoln and London: University of Nebraska Press.

Iyengar, S. (1991), *Is Anyone Responsible? How Television Frames Political Issues*, Chicago: University of Chicago Press.

Jenkins, H. (1992), *Textual Poachers*, New York: Routledge.

Klein, N. (2001), *No Logo*, London: Harper Collins.

Lacey, N. (2000), *Narrative and Genre: Key Concepts in Media Studies*, Basingstoke and London: Macmillan, now Palgrave Macmillan.

McCullagh, C. (2002), *Media Power: A Sociological Introduction*, Basingstoke: Palgrave Macmillan.

McQuail, D. (1992 (1983)), *Mass Communication Theory: An Introduction*, 2nd edn, London: Sage.

Morley, D. (1980), *The 'Nationwide' Audience*, London: BFI.

Radway, J. (1987), *Reading the Romance: Women, Patriarchy, and Popular Literature*, London: Verso.

Scheufele, D. A. (1999), 'Framing as a Theory of Media Effects', *Journal of Communication*, Winter: 103–22.

Thornham, S. and Purvis, T. (2004), *Television Drama: Theories and Identities*, Basingstoke: Palgrave Macmillan.

Watson, J. (1998), *Media Communication: An Introduction to Theory and Process*, Basingstoke and London: Macmillan, now Palgrave Macmillan.

Williams, R. (1965), *The Long Revolution*, Harmondsworth: Penguin.

Williams, R. (1988; 1976), *Keywords: A Vocabulary of Culture and Society*, London: Fontana.

USEFUL INTERNET RESOURCES FOR MEDIA AND CULTURAL STUDIES

http://www.aber.ac.uk/media/
http://www.cultsock.ndirect.co.uk/MUHome/cshtml/
http://www.scils.rutgers.edu/~favretto/media.html
www.theory.org.uk/
www.michaelmoore.com/

INDEX